Magdalen Smith is National ministry in the Church of En̄g ~~~~ ~~~ ~ p̄r̄īēs̄t̄ īn̄ t̄h̄ē D̄īōc̄ēs̄ē ōf Guildford. She has been involved in the ministry of vocation and spirituality for many years and has a background in the visual arts. A retreat leader and spiritual director, she is the author of five books, including *Steel Angels: The personal qualities of a priest*; *Fragile Mystics: Reclaiming a prayerful life*; and, co-written with Bishop Andrew Watson, *The Great Vocations Conversation*.

THE GRACE-FILLED WILDERNESS

A journey through Lent

Magdalen Smith

First published in Great Britain in 2019

Society for Promoting Christian Knowledge
36 Causton Street
London SW1P 4ST
www.spck.org.uk

British Library Cataloguing-in-Publication Data
A catalogue record for this book is available from the British Library

ISBN 978–0–281–08010–6
eBook ISBN 978–0–281–08011–3

1 3 5 7 9 10 8 6 4 2

Typeset by Manila Typesetting Company
Printed in Great Britain by Ashford Colour Press

eBook by Manila Typesetting Company

Produced on paper from sustainable forests

For the Diocese of Chester

Contents

Contents

Contents

After Easter

Acknowledgements

A special thank you to Ian and Georgina Watmore, who have aided the writing of this book by providing a generous and tranquil space.

Introduction: the grace-filled wilderness

It's 3.00 a.m. and I'm wide awake. As I lie in the dark, all the worries and complications of my life crowd in, the possibility of sleep feeling more unlikely as the minutes tick by. Over the last 18 months, life has been complicated. I am living away from my husband, who has taken a new job two hundred miles away, while our two children stay with me in order to complete an important stage in their education. Thanks to the generosity of friends, I'm living in a beautiful but borrowed house, surrounded by stuff that isn't mine. The three of us grapple with the slow extraction of our emotional and physical life from the area that has been our home for the best part of ten years.

The middle of the night is when the demons get to me, the time when it is physically darkest. I wake and feel suffocated by the cares and concerns of my life, the larger challenges as well as the minutiae, which press in, and I am tempted in that moment to dispense with everything that feels like an additional pressure. Living away from the person I love most in the world, the juggling of my children's needs and the start of a stimulating but demanding new job myself, with multiple deadlines, have pushed me to my limits, as well as a multitude of other arrangements that need organizing.

Perhaps most of us have been here – a time when we feel incapacitated with worry or upset, and we feel alone and sometimes desperate. At this moment, I pray that this mental tumult will cease and that God will enfold me in his powerful peace, for I know that I cannot carry all of this in my strength alone. Grace, it seems, is the admittance of this – at 3.00 a.m., the wilderness hour. But if I can find a way to let go, then a peace flows through my mind, heart and body as I somehow give up the managing of my life, even temporarily, reminding myself that grace comes in the form of kind friends, the taking of each day at a time and the deep belief that I and those I love are deeply loved and mysteriously held in God.

Lent is a season that occupies the Church year for approximately six weeks before the glorious rays of Easter shine into the gloom once again. Traditionally understood as a 'penitential' season, Lent encourages us to reflect on our own fallible state, our own fragility as human people, the fact of our own need for God. Lent can be used to reflect on the difficult things in our lives as well as life's problematic questions.

But Lent is often more than this too – it can signify a state of existence, an entrenched mindset and sometimes even a way of life. Lent can creep up on us unawares as we find that we are, without realizing it, wrapped in its shadows. Lent can happen in January or July, at Christmas or in the summer holidays. Lent is a spiritual state, and it can be a metaphor for those most harsh, most inexplicable times when we understand that life is tough through our living of it. We feel the deep pain of a situation, whether our own or another's, disappointment, a feeling of being trapped or when a hunger is not satisfied by what we think will fill it. Lent is when we cannot seem to shake off a deep-seated desolation which dumps itself like a heavy weight at the pit of our soul. It is when we are neither here nor there, an absence when we are forever waiting for something to happen, but we know not when.

At the beginning of this season we traditionally remember Jesus going into the wilderness of the Judean desert. Three of the Gospels tell this story. Matthew's account describes Jesus as being 'led' into this place to be tempted by the devil. Fast-forward 40 days and the devil (however we understand this) reappears to do his utmost to tempt Jesus with all those human temptations most of us are all too familiar with. Whether we read this as historical reality, metaphor or both, it is worth reflecting on the 'space' of the wilderness and what Jesus goes through in order to provide such a feisty resistance to the luring charms of human appetites and folly presented to him so attractively by Satan himself.

There are not many places in our lives where we would encounter such vast nothingness, or where we would voluntarily choose to take ourselves away from all the comfort and consolation that surround us. We are people who both think and feel; the wilderness is potentially a place where both have nowhere to be satisfied but still have to be dealt with. Jesus would have to reflect on the purpose of his existence, on his own potential success or failure, on his popularity, on the resistance that he is to face, and all of this amid loneliness and hunger.

The Christian journey is not easy, precisely because it invites us all to respond well to those most difficult of temptations and experiences. It is not easy because it asks us to try to make sense of such places when we inadvertently find ourselves somewhere dark. It is not easy because it asks us to stay in those hard places as well as to go beyond them to search for hope.

At the beginning of Matthew 4 we are told that Jesus is led into the wilderness *by the Spirit*, and at the end of the ordeal that angels minister to him. Mark's brief account (Mark 1.12–13) is linked with Jesus' baptism and he is led into the desert with words of love resounding in his ears: 'You are my Son, the Beloved; with you I am well pleased.' God does not leave Jesus just with desolation or to be tried beyond his means; he is *with him* throughout. Wherever our own wildernesses might be it, they are not simply negative places, as St John of the Cross and the other apophatic mystics discovered when they courageously faced the dark night. In this life, it is easy for us to feel lost, to forget that we have Jesus to recalibrate our lives, like a spiritual compass.

Jesus leaves the desert to begin his decisive and demanding journey to his passion and death, with sureness of heart and foot that he will enter Jerusalem, even though he has identified it as a city that 'kills the prophets and stones those sent to it' (Matthew 23.37). At this stage in his life, Jesus walks right into the world's sin and evil, but it is this trajectory that brings the joy and new life of the resurrection.

The desert, or wilderness, then, must not be understood as something entirely negative but as a place of discipline, development and honing. For Jesus, it is a place of encounter – a time when he comes face to face with himself as a human being and a place where he sees beyond his humanity to the reality of who God is and what is being asked of him.

Our own lives are rarely made up of times when we feel on a 100 per cent undiluted high, or the opposite of 100 per cent despair. Rather, life is made up of a duality that is connected, where both hope and pain are intertwined. On most days there is always something to feel grateful for, to be joyful about even in the midst of the stuff we are bearing which is problematic and sore. In the wilderness, Satan as well as the angels are there; the Passion Narrative has friends betraying Jesus as well as carrying his cross and wiping his face; Good Friday is followed by Easter Day. Our lives, as Jesus' life, are a mixed bag.

If we are committed to following Jesus, we too must be prepared to be seriously changed maybe many times over. Our call is also to be people who can inject hope into the bleakest and most desperate of situations in a cynical and weary world. As Rowan Williams puts it in *Being Disciples*:

> The disciple is not there to jot down ideas and then go away and think about them. The disciple is where he or she is in order to be changed; so that the way in which he or she sees and experiences the whole world changes. Disciples watch, they remain alert, attentive, watching symbolic acts as well as listening for instructive words; watching the actions that give the clue to how reality is being reorganized around Jesus.[1]

Reality is reorganized around Jesus primarily through love. Love leads him from a place of emptiness into the sordidness and exuberance of human life. It also leads him to a place of service and to be close to his Father, who is the source of all love. In the wilderness, Jesus must be deeply attentive to his own inner processes, to his internal and external demons, who try to mould him into a distorted human being and to knock him off course. Jesus is pulled and pushed by societal forces and by those he encounters, just as we are, but his time in the desert is a time when he refocuses so that no other god is able to exert influence over the primary aim of his life, that of love and service to the world. Experiencing and surviving the wilderness is about a recognition that we are primarily shaped by Christ and that all other relationships and preoccupations may prove to be distractions if they begin to eclipse this focus in our lives. It is these distractions that often become the idols, the issues and the obsessions we overly worry about and become consumed by, especially at 3.00 a.m.

Each of the chapters in this book provides an opportunity to use Lent to reflect on the significance of Jesus' wilderness experience, as well as on the momentous days of Holy Week. Themes that are both ancient and acutely contemporary are identified and explored through the biblical text, story, the visual arts and film. Each chapter also contains an offering of redemption and hope, which forms part of the culmination of the Passion Narrative as Easter returns. The gospel asks of us hard things at times, but even in disorientation and displacement we can still feel the Spirit's soothing, can still regain our spiritual equilibrium, can still be drawn by the vision and fulfilment God has for us.

The Christian life is essentially one that is always lived in hope as well as joy. It is a life in which we are asked to bravely face the times of difficulty and temptation, always trusting that God's grace is ever present, that the sun and stars are there behind the clouds and that, like a kaleidoscope full of broken glass, the message of Easter reconfigures our humanity with restored colour and strength.

WEEK 1

Introduction: appetite

The cursing of the fig tree
(Mark 11.12–14, 20–25)

Vine leaves and pine nuts and raisins and rice
Goat's cheese and oranges, apricots, spice . . .
Mullet, merluzza, salt-lemons, anise,
Honey and wine at the feast . . .
At the feast.[1]

No person is free who is not master of himself.
(Epictetus, AD *c.*50–135)

Returning after a long walk in the early autumn, and not having eaten since breakfast, I am hungry. Being hungry is not a bad thing. One of many appetites, it reminds us that we have physical needs as human people, and that at a basic level we become vulnerable if we do not eat a healthy and nourishing diet. Used to living in a society where we have every opportunity to consume food, many of us have forgotten what a hunger pang is.

Mark 11.12 reminds us that Jesus gets hungry too as, after much demanding ministry and the jubilant entry into Jerusalem, he looks for what is instantly available and tries to forage for figs. Unyielding, the poor plant gets cursed, shrivels and dies.

Jesus uses the story to teach his disciples about the power of faith and prayer. But, interestingly, in between his command and its explanation comes the passage often referred to as the cleansing of the temple. Jesus goes to the Jewish temple and drives out those who are sullying its holy ground. Within its sanctified walls, traders and moneylenders have succumbed to what amounts to bad appetite, the temptation to be greedy. Corruption is rife as businessmen line their pockets and exploit the poor.

Lent brings the opportunity to contemplate Jesus practising tremendous self-discipline with regard to his physical appetite as he wanders around a desert space with no nutrition whatsoever – for 40 days. Christians can be witnesses to the fact that the appetites we have are essentially good things, especially when they are directed towards God. The food and drink we choose, eat and produce are first and foremost grace-filled and bountiful gifts, elements in our lives that, although necessary, provide joy, sustenance and often companionship which go way beyond the physical upkeep of our bodies.

We can also be good stewards of these, reintroducing a voluntary discipline that can be physically as well as spiritually beneficial. Such discipline strengthens our resolve not to be defined by our appetites, past or present, whatever they may be. It refreshes our knowledge that although the food we choose from the supermarket shelves seems readily available, the reality is that we rely on many other people to eat each day. The consumer choices we make have a direct impact on food producers in both the national as well as the global marketplace.

There is no room to take the moral high ground here, for we are all people of physical desires and weaknesses. People of faith and none struggle with getting a handle on their appetites. Most of us have our weaknesses: overeating, drinking too much, maybe struggling with sexual gratification; as well as these days other appetites absent from the biblical text, such as shopping, gambling or technology.

The hopeful film, *A Street Cat Named Bob* (2016), tells the true story of James Bowen, a recovering drug addict whose adoption by a ginger tom enables him to finally kick his drug habit and earn significant money as a busker. There are scenes in the film where James is continually tempted to get a heroin fix, lured by fellow addicts. One gritty scene describes in graphic reality the physical hellishness of the attempt to conquer heroin and its antidotes.

Succumbing to appetite without discipline is a natural human tendency in us all. When we are broken, feeling low or rejected or even working too hard, it's easy to turn to chocolate, wine, porn, nicotine – whatever lights our fire and makes us feel instantly better.

Tobias Jones, a Christian and the initiator of the Windsor Hill Wood Community in Somerset, describes the experience of living and working among people whose appetites have become detrimental to them, and the place community plays in their healing. Even with the subtler addictions such as shopping or gambling, he says:

> In a dry house, you start to notice the unhealthy consumption of coffee or sugar and, especially, the twitchy dependence on electronic gadgetry. I wondered why recovery invariably takes place in a communal setting. Most recovering addicts say that being alone is like being behind enemy lines. It's obvious, but recovery's bound to be easier when you are surrounded by people trying to help you beat an addiction.[2]

Jones observes what we already know: that addiction is a spiritual malady, that a lack of control over appetite can signify the fact that 'family, tribal, cultural and spiritual ties have been severed. We are dislocated, isolated and atomized beings who have become, thanks to super-speed capitalism and acute consumer competitiveness, incredibly individualistic.'[3]

Essentially, appetite is a good desire, but it can swiftly escalate into obsession, addiction and unhealthy cravings. Set firmly in the account of the temptations of Jesus as well as in many other places in the Bible, an understanding of appetite is always placed alongside discipline and self-control. What happens to our bodies physically has inevitable spiritual consequences.

1 Corinthians 6 has the familiar verses:

> Or do you not know that your body is a temple of the Holy Spirit within you, which you have from God, and that you are not your own? For you were bought with a price; therefore, glorify God in your body.
> (1 Corinthians 6.19–20)

In these verses there is wisdom and grace, suggesting that in every aspect of life which is given to us as a 'gift', even our bodies are vehicles that potentially point to something else: that which is God. Our bodies are intricate and precious, communicators of living lives filled and fuelled by the Holy Spirit of God. For others to see this we must get our attitudes to appetite – any appetite – in check, in order to live both celebratory as well as disciplined lives.

This chapter provides reflections on what might be described as a journey through **appetite**. As people inspired by hope, who feel something of a responsibility to others who provide so much of our food across the globe, how do we respond to the continuous scandal of **hunger**? What about the physical and spiritual concept of **fasting**, which is reappearing in some contemporary diet regimes, and the rediscovery of its enormous benefits for our holistic wellbeing? In contrast, there is the challenge of **feasting** in an age in which plenty and choice seem never-ending possibilities for us as consumers. With this comes the ambiguous idea of **excess**, which can imply both a positive and negative understanding related to appetite, both of which can be found in the Bible, along with the formulation of a spiritually life-giving and grace-filled approach to food, **bread for the world**, which is inextricably connected to the most symbolic of meals, the Eucharist.

Hunger

The Israelites are fed manna and quails in the desert
(Exodus 16)

We must eat to live and not live to eat.
(Michel Quoist, 1918–97)[1]

We live in a surprisingly hungry world. It is a global problem from which the world will never be completely free. As people who understand food as gift, it seems scandalous and frustrating that so many regularly still have too little to eat while a smaller proportion of the planet live in uninterrupted plenty. Unless our jobs give us a genuine platform of influence to respond to humanitarian crises, most of us easily become emotionally anaesthetized when famine hits the media, especially when our own stomachs are so often filled.

Yet stories of hunger abound daily. In January 2017 the Bishop of Madagascar reported that starving people in his community had resorted to eating locusts to try to survive, with one young man collapsing during a confirmation service.[2] The tragedy is that God's resourceful earth has always been bountiful enough to feed its ever-burgeoning population, but the prospect of fair distribution is not at all likely, for complex reasons. An area's specific agricultural and climatic conditions, as well as its political and economic stability, all contribute to whether somewhere is a hungry place. A recent UN report, 'The State of Food Security and Nutrition in the World 2017', states that world hunger is on the rise, with 815 million people now hungry, including millions of children who risk long-term malnutrition. This is an increase of 38 million from the previous year, a result largely owing to the proliferation of violent conflicts and climate-related disasters, according to the report.[3] Even in wealthy Britain, the rise of the food bank has demonstrated that many people simply do not have enough money to feed their families properly.

A definition of hunger is 'a feeling of discomfort or weakness caused by lack of food, coupled with the desire to eat', 'a severe lack of food', including the scarcity of food in a country, and 'a strong desire or craving'.[4] In spiritual terms, hunger describes an aching gap, a yearning for something that is not in place in our lives and which does not satisfy us, like the feeling of being unloved. Hunger accelerates the concept of appetite, changing it from a natural feeling to something unhealthy and sometimes life-threatening. It is not merely a few stomach rumblings but the inability, through circumstances beyond an individual's control, to live a fulfilled life, not only with a balanced diet but also with all those elements in place that sustain our well-being.

Yet hunger is biblical. Jesus is described as 'hungry' when he finally emerges from his wilderness experience (Luke 4.2). In Genesis 25, Esau is described as hungry after his hunt and demands some red stew. Luke 16 describes the poor beggar, Lazarus, who longs to satisfy his ongoing hunger from scraps that fell from the rich man's table.

Food is not only physically vital, it has emotional and spiritual implications too, back then as well as now, of comfort and reassurance. Jesus tells those fretting around the daughter of Jairus to give her something to eat (Luke 8.55). Physical food is symbolic of the bigger picture of God as Jesus invites his disciples to partake in something that is a symbol of *him*, his life of sacrifice and redemption, and inspires them to do the same.

The story of the Israelites in the Sinai desert in Exodus 16 feels epic in its proportion. Like so many today, a large group of people have left their home country and a deeply oppressive situation. Becoming migratory refugees, they are vulnerable, and they look to their leader Moses to be sustained.

The situation does not bode well; in the preceding chapter, after three days desperately thirsty, they find water at Marah, but it tastes bitter and impure. Hunger brings desperation and anger, with the Israelites railing against their newfound freedom, remembering that even in oppression their bellies were full. God sends protein in the form of quails (small birds that could land near the coast of Sinai) and 'bread' in the form of manna (probably the resin that seeps out in abundance from certain brambles in the desert and tastes like biscuits made with honey) as food for the people.

Verses 17 and 18 are telling, describing that some gathered more than others but 'when they measured it with an omer, those who gathered much had nothing over, and those who gathered little had no shortage; they gathered as much as each of them needed'. This is an interesting comment amid a situation of crisis – that somehow God inspires the people to take what each family needs and no more, an ideal principle which, if applied globally, would have some consequence in terms of the distribution of resources for all.

We are told too that some of the Israelites, tempted to store up enough food for tomorrow, discover that this is not God's intention as the food turns rotten. All points to a new trust in a God who will provide in times of desperation. Interestingly, on the Sabbath day food is not to be found because of the firm command to rest.

The chapter ends with two litres of manna being kept in a jar as a recognition and thanksgiving for all God has provided for them.

What, then, is our response as Christian people to ever-present global hunger and in situations where God does not seemingly provide enough to save lives? Hunger is never God's intention, but complex factors of climate change, distributional logistics and political complexities make it often hard to ease. Aid agencies and our own financial help are perhaps today's manna and quails. Grace can flow too through solidarity with the hungry with prayer as its partner. Prayer reminds us that the food we choose and eat often has significant implications for others on the planet and, as people of plenteous resources, we can use our time and energy to play our part to alleviate local and worldwide hunger.

Supporters of Tearfund eat porridge for breakfast and rice and beans for lunch and dinner for one week during Lent, to raise money for people who are suffering from food shortage. The challenge brings to light the sparse subsistence-level diet of people in countries like Ethiopia, Malawi, Southern Sudan and Kenya and seeks to raise money for the agency's projects in the area.[5] Ronald Sider, an American theologian and social activist, talks about God requiring us to radically transform economic relationships among his people globally and states that the division between rich and poor within the body of Christ is a major hindrance to evangelism.[6] Grace manifests itself as we refuse to accept the outrage of hunger and as we work continually, in whatever ways possible, to alleviate it.

Fast

Jesus fasting in the wilderness
(Matthew 4.1–11)

When people pray and fast there's an increase of Holy Spirit activity.
(Mike Bickle)[1]

Fasting is in. It's January, and the most recent weight-loss television show, *Lose Weight for Good*, is delivered by the celebrity chef Tom Kerridge, who in three years has shifted an impressive 12 stone of weight. A year or two ago, Dr Michael Mosley and others hit the bookshop shelves with their 'Fast Diet', a way of life that aimed at stabilizing a person's weight by eating just a quarter of the usual daily calorie intake two days a week. People swore by it, and for many it worked because its psychology suggested that there was no 'diet' involved and that reasonable eating would happen on the remaining five days. But many also warmed to the old-fashioned idea of fasting, promoted by Mosley, as a discipline that reaps long-term health benefits, enabling the body to rejuvenate itself as well as lessening mental and physical health problems later in life.

I'm watching Kerridge's series this year too because I enjoy programmes about food, and in last year's series one of the participants was the Revd Jenny Ellis, a chaplain at Bucks New University. She tells viewers that in the Bible there is quite a lot about both fasting and feasting; it's just that she's 'not very good at the fasting part!'[2]

This hits the nail on the head. Fasting in the western Christian tradition has seen a steady decline as a faith practice over recent years. Worse still, it is gently sneered at in a society, and often a Church, that worships at the altar of continuous choice. We cannot bear feeling that we are prohibited from doing something, that we can't communicate, can't buy or eat what we want when we want to. Fasting is unpopular in this respect partly because it smacks of a dour discipline associated with the worst kind of killjoy religion. Yet in contemporary culture, fasting abounds in healthy eating programmes and literature.

It's interesting that the spirituality of this and the faith history behind it are now rarely mentioned. Yet within Islam and in other religions it is taken extremely seriously. The importance of Ramadan within Islam came home to me when I had a spontaneous conversation with a Muslim employee at my bank. She described being unable to eat or drink anything until sundown – and she was still smiling. Perhaps fasting is eased when it becomes a communal activity, when there is an understood focus and the focus points away from ourselves. Periods of fasting naturally flow into periods of feasting, as properly undertaken they complement one another as Advent moves into Christmas and as Lent moves into Easter.

Alone in the wilderness, Jesus prepares himself to be confronted by his own physicality, his human frailty and the immensity of the great power that appetite has over us all. Forty days and nights is a long time. But Jesus refuses to turn three hard, stony rocks into delicious yeasty loaves, not just through simple willpower but through a spiritual discipline that could only come from God. When Jesus says 'no' to the power of evil he is saying 'yes' to living a disciplined physical life; a life which, when lived well and fuelled by the Spirit, is transformed into a state of joyful 'enough'.

In our often-satiated world, being physically hungry has become unknown territory, on the whole. It seems a frightening thing for us to be hungry. Jesus fasts to strengthen his resolve to see him along the path he believes he must walk down. Faith, prayer and fasting form both a temporary barricade and a personal and symbolic battle against cosmic evil, which have eternal significance. Martin Thornton writes:

> Self-denial for the love of God, however seemingly trivial, may take on the character of Our Lord's 40 days, as preparation for the fight against sin, which is still part of the vicarious principle and which, within sacred humanity, has eternal significance.[3]

Food is only the incidental appetite the devil focuses on. Today, we live with other elements that we consider essential for our survival – electronic media being one. In the wilderness, Jesus is stripped of things that could take up his time – in this case, eating. Instead, resisting what his body craves, he embraces the space of nothingness, immersing into a deeper spiritually to hone himself.

One new spiritual discipline is to analyse what have become our appetites and to think about why we make certain choices. It is in part caused by the bombardment of advertising that tells us we're worth it, that somehow we deserve it and need to be continuously rewarded and satiated. With this we contemplate what freedom really means for us and whether having a multiplicity of choice is so important. We need to analyse what is behind our desires to discover whether it is possible to move towards a deeper rhythm which becomes part of a more considered and compassionate way of understanding our appetites. This is to live with the contradiction of discovering that we can be free from being enslaved by our appetites by formulating a disciplined life. Perhaps this is why Jesus needs such a long time in the wilderness to reconnect with this – God's divine as well as his own human trajectory.

Jesus' own waiting to eat until he leaves the wilderness is an indication that it can be good to say no or even to wait, to make decisive as well as prayerful decisions about what we consume and to contemplate what we are consumed by. In biblical typology the wilderness can symbolize contemplative silence, and so we can use the season of Lent as a space of non-consumption, fasting from food, technology, business, even sex, to pray more and to embrace the space that opens in our lives. The discipline that goes hand in hand with fasting is and always has been a grace-filled quality, deeply biblical and firmly rooted in the Christian tradition. We are privileged with opportunity – to live as healthy and Spirit-filled people who can find the strength of witness to live against the flow of continuous consumption.

Feast

The prodigal son
(Luke 15.11–32)

There was salad sprinkled with fresh flowers – Isabel said they were baby pansies, nasturtium and angelica. The spread included plates of artisan cheeses and raw and grilled vegetables, big chafing dishes of fragrant casseroles, berries and apples with a variety of sauces, an array of local wines and water from Calistoga. The abundance was almost overwhelming to Tess.
(Susan Wiggs in *The Apple Orchard*)[1]

Feast is not so much an event as an attitude. Many in the western hemisphere live perpetually in a state of feast. What might years ago have been considered food for a special occasion or food that marks a significant event is now continuously available, should our bank balances permit. Our lives are flooded with an exotic and mouth-watering variety of food, food programmes, food literature and advertising, a carnival of deliciousness that is designed to tantalize our taste buds and make celebrity chefs of us all.

But genuine feasts are still present in our lives, thank goodness, and symbolize celebration, joyfulness, anticipation and achievement. Feast lies within the coming together of people who love one another; it is often is about gratitude and occasionally about reconciliation, as is demonstrated in the story of the wayward prodigal son. In this passage, food is contrasted sharply, as the resources squandered so swiftly and intensively by the younger son result in a rapid change in lifestyle. He is initially unappreciative of the precious inheritance he receives and he ends up grubbing around with the pigs.

The text mentions his physical hunger, that he is so famished he would literally eat the pods given to the animals in his care. Hunger sharpens the mind and the senses, enabling this young man to realize the folly of his ways and to yearn to return to the security of his father's house – and presumably its full larder. He returns tentatively, genuinely happy just to live with his father's servants and prepared to relinquish the privileges of a son. But his father is having none of it; at a distance the wayward son is a sight for sore eyes, and he is welcomed home wholeheartedly. The return of he who was so lost, a family reunited, a transformed life, is here understood as an event that warrants a feast. Food – here the calf that has been fattened for a special occasion – is quickly slaughtered to create a banquet to which presumably the whole household is invited. It is just the elder son, shrivelled by jealously, who refuses to join the celebration.

Feast, more than anything, is about the approach we take to food. Meaning an 'abundant meal', with its Latin root *festum* linking it to joy and the idea of the festival, it is a periodical time of celebration to mark a religious or community event. Depending on our perspective, even the simplest of fare has the potential to become something celebratory.

The film *Paddington 2* (2017) has the nation's favourite bear being falsely accused of the crime of stealing a valuable antique book. Poor Paddington is put in jail, the only cuddly creature among some hard-nosed criminals, including the cook, Knuckles McGinty, brilliantly played by Brendan Gleeson. Sick of the monotony of stodgy porridge, Paddington softens the cook by teaching him to make marmalade, which becomes quickly incorporated into his signature sandwiches, eaten at breakfast each morning. The inclusion of sugar sweetens the hearts and attitudes of those inside, and the dreary prison canteen is fantastically imagined as a retro tearoom with an array of sumptuous patisserie. Feast reimagines the drab and ordinary, just from the taste of marmalade.

Feast here is linked with familiarity; it is what Paddington knows and the food he offers as a gift. This simple foodstuff is the catalyst that transforms the hardness of the terrifying Knuckles, the larger-than-life comic bully. It is this that boosts morale and brings the inmates of the prison together.

The concept of the feast, then, is a communal one, linked to the word for festival. It is quite difficult to have a feast alone and enjoy it. Good bread and good cheese can be a feast as much as a dinner in a posh restaurant.

For Christians, feast is about a deep appreciation of the gift of food, and a recognition that those who have produced what we eat, both near and far, are spiritually connected to us and that we accept some responsibility for them. Feast is about approaching what we eat with a natural respect as well as a delight in the beautiful occasion of the banquet, big or small. Feast is getting the balance right between fasting and moderation, to enjoy a treat.

When Jesus inhabits spaces where food and drink are involved, he uses his God-given powers to redirect the situations, moving them from anxiety to enjoyment. He changes water into wine at the wedding in Cana when those responsible are worried; he multiplies the simple fare of loaves and fishes for the hungry crowd at the feeding of the five thousand; he cooks the tired disciples a breakfast of grilled fish on the beach. The presence of Jesus creates feast, and there is something about locally sourced, lovingly produced food set in an atmosphere where people are genuinely welcomed that potentially and mysteriously recreates this in any setting.

Tertullian, the North African Church Father, pointed out that the Christian name for 'feast' also explains the reason for it – *agape* in Greek, meaning 'love'. We cannot, therefore, have feast without love if we are followers of Jesus, and it is this element that makes any meal, be it simple or culinarily complex, into a meal that contains a sense of the holy. The father in Luke 15 is overcome with compassion for his wayward younger son who stumbles, mud-caked and despairing, into his arms.

The restaurateur Bill Sewell, responsible for initiating several acclaimed cafés in churches and cathedrals, says:

> Food is a spiritual issue. One of the things we are is what we put in our mouths. Eating should bind us together – but at the same time, the division between filling ourselves with junk food and feasting on proper freshly cooked food is one of the great social dividers of our age, and probably most other ages too.[2]

Feast, as Jesus so clearly demonstrated, is about using good food on opportune occasions to cross those divides through the invitation of hospitality. Lent is an opportunity to do this as well as to hold back from the instantaneous availability of luxury food, to appreciate in a new way the preciousness of what we eat and drink, where it comes from and who produces it. Feast is the natural progression from fast, but only retains power if we have undergone something of a journey of physical and spiritual discipline. Feast is the integration of all we hold necessary and deeply love as human people. It is the combination of nutritious and delectable food and drink and the company of others, both known and new, that becomes a means of grace.

Excess

The feeding of the five thousand
(Matthew 14.13–21)

Use, do not abuse . . . neither abstinence nor excess ever renders
man happy.
(Voltaire, 1694–1778)

Jesus is trying to restore his tired soul, but the crowds have followed
him nevertheless. He cannot escape from their demands and he
is ever generous. Depleted of strength, the text tells us he draws on
his deep compassion for those who need him and delivers yet again
the elements they crave – his time, words of wisdom and healing.
Tiredness compounds yet more tiredness, and towards the end of
the day the disciples, protective of their master, diplomatically tell
him to wrap things up. In the middle of nowhere, they don't want
the responsibility of 'hangry' people – people who get angry and
emotional because they are hungry – so want to send them back to
the town before things get out of hand. Turning their challenge right
around, Jesus tells them to feed the people *themselves* rather than send
them away. For feeding is a sign of God's excessive and continuous
hospitality, his love and kindness to his people wherever they are.

The disciples find a laughable offering for the needs of such
a large crowd – five loaves and two fishes; food that would have
constituted an average peasant's lunch. The feeding is the only
miracle story within the New Testament that is recorded in each
of the four Gospels, suggesting that it is of special significance.
Various interpretations as to how such a huge crowd of people are
fed abound – perhaps a youthful sharing which inspires generosity,

or Jesus' blessing which miraculously magnifies the amount of food and means that every stomach is filled. Here is a sign of the immediate needs of the present combined with looking towards the future 'messianic banquet' when the world just might look more equal, more just, where the hungry are fed in every way.

This event, like many in the Gospels, acts as a premonitory episode, hastening on the less happy events at the end of Jesus' life. As at the Last Supper, Jesus here takes, blesses, breaks and shares the food. Jesus' presence also becomes the secret ingredient whereby the spiritual as well as the physical appetites of many are satisfied, provided by a sacrificial offering, the giving away of one person's lunch and, later, bread as a symbol of his own body at the Last Supper. Matthew's version of the story focuses on the physical needs of the people, in contrast to John's version, where it is the *words* of Jesus that provide true nourishment (John 6.1–13, 35–63).

Excess in the Bible is ambiguous. The natural world blooms to produce good things – oil, figs, wheat, wine – all seen as gifts from God to his people. In today's world too, much vegetable produce over the summer means a communal sharing; a prolific orchard full of trees groaning with apples gives animals a chance to eat. Yet greed, drunkenness and the amassing of wealth are understood as abuses of divine gifts. In Luke 12.13–21, the rich farmer building larger and larger barns is assessed as foolish because he does not live to enjoy his stash of superfluous crops. But there is also great excess in the expensive fragrance the unnamed woman pours all over Jesus in preparation for his death, for which she is recognized as performing a wonderful ritual of deep significance (John 12.1–8).

Excess in terms of waste has always been considered detrimental in many cultures and faiths. Excess is something often offered to the gods or to the poor, and what matters is that the produce of the created world is not cast aside casually or without due reverence. Recently in our overflowing world of too much, we have begun to question the profligate waste that comes with excess – food rejected by supermarkets simply because of its shape, the attractively packaged and managed food left to rot in landfills because of the overconscientiousness regarding sell-by dates. Excess can signify exuberance, celebration or humanity's greed, an obsessive need to have maximum choice. The infamous Imelda Marcos, wife of the Philippine dictator Ferdinand Marcos, is reputedly said to have once spent more than $2,000 on chewing gum at San Francisco International Airport, and her collection of more than a thousand pairs of shoes became a symbol in the twentieth century of reckless excess at the expense of the poor of that country.

At the end of the feeding of the five thousand, 12 baskets of excess food are collected, but it is not clear what happens to this food. As readers, we do not often dwell on these leftovers. Scholars often interpret them as symbols of the 12 tribes of Israel, while others have suggested that in fact 12 baskets of leftovers from such a huge crowd is not, in fact, a great deal. The margins are slim, as God provides but not with a superabundance, implying that we, as stewards of the earth, need to be careful in our production as well as our consumption of food and goods.

The very fact that food is gathered up surely means it is understood to be important, that somehow it will be reused. During Lent, this fact takes on special significance as we reflect on our own attitude to excess, what we consume and how we use and process leftover food and the things we no longer want or need. John's version of the story makes explicit the idea that the bread used to feed the people is to be understood as the body of Jesus, Jesus himself saying, 'I am the bread of life' and 'the bread of God is that which comes down from heaven and gives life to the world' (John 6.35, 33). If this is true, then the 'excess' is also Jesus' 'body', to be treated with respect, to be used to feed the world. Excess is to be treated carefully and with gratitude.

The Real Junk Food Project initiative, founded by Adam Smith, is now a worldwide phenomenon, with excess food produced mostly by supermarkets being rechannelled to construct delicious fresh food for anyone who wants to eat it. There are now many Real Junk Food Café Projects globally, producing nutritious meals for anyone whose imagination is captured by this brilliant concept.[1] Smith hopes that this is the beginning of a global movement: to end food waste and to use excess for good. Interestingly, he wants to help people franchise this idea – the only rules are that you must feed everyone, not just poor people, and customers should pay what they feel the meal is worth, volunteering labour and skills if their financial resources are not sufficient.

Here is a contemporary feeding of the five thousand story, identifying that we will perhaps always live in a world where there is excess because God provides for his children richly. Jesus is a man who manages to feast well while at the same time pointing to a God who needs his children to (urgently) care about the life of the earth and to feed those who need good sustenance of every kind.

Bread for the world

The Last Supper
(Matthew 26.17–25)

I've learned that the table is a powerful symbol of a world put right. At the table you look people in the eyes. The surface of the table is level. It's a levelling act. It creates an environment whereby you reach your hands into the same pot, take from the same food, to sustain your lives in the same way. You have come in need of the same thing, and you get that need met by performing the same actions at the same time.
(Ryan Cook)[1]

I am writing this reflection in early January, the happy satisfaction of Christmas still a vivid memory of the recent past. Christmas lunch, actually just a glorified roast dinner, is a meal many of us stress about. As we yearn for the perfect atmosphere of full bellies and contented relatives, there remains an underlying tension that all should be well. Perhaps this is the reality of most of the meals we host for others as we worry about whether the food is delicious – or at the very least acceptable; we hope that our guests get on with one another, and we are anxious that our unpolitically correct uncle won't overstep the mark and upset our prickly neighbour.

Like many meals, the Last Supper sees a host seated at a table with a bunch of friends, here set in a borrowed room. Like Christmas, this meal is associated with a religious festival, the insistent tradition of Passover for which the disciples have gathered. Around the table is no holy huddle, as Jesus states that he knows one of his 'friends' will betray him. There is outrage; the disciples

23

are described as 'greatly distressed' (Matthew 26.22), and confusion moves through the table like a breeze ruffling the tablecloth.

This is no idealized meal, for gathered here are the weak (who could be strong), the traitors (who should be faithful friends), the self-righteous (who could be humble) and the dense (who should, by this time, understand the implications of what is going on). But the table takes no prisoners as it provides an opportunity where all this is exposed. It is ultimately a sacramental and unifying place for all this human failure, ensuring still that this notorious band of Christ's followers are given the opportunity to witness to the deep symbolism, through food, of Jesus' message to them and thus to the world. The table, the food and even the company are the ingredients that make this event, as potentially every meal that is shared, an unconventional means of grace.

Jesus delivers an uncomfortable message. Here are no cosy reminiscences of past life, no 'Do you remember the time when . . .?' memories. Instead he gives to his motley group a story that tells of the sacrifice he is about to make, the offering of his body and blood, to be completely beaten and broken, for the sake of others.

The table is a place where the most radical and momentous sign of God's inclusive love and gospel of grace is played out. The table, the altar of our every Sunday, is a symbol of what followers of Christ are challenged to think about putting in place in their own lives. The table is a place where those who know each other and those who do not yet feel included can come and gather. The table is where they can witness the mystery of something momentous – that God wants all people to be fed physically through good food as well as through inclusive companionship.

Ryan Cook describes, in his blog, an event that he has run for several years out of his home in Liverpool. Every Monday evening, he and his wife host an 'open invitation' meal for friends, neighbours and strangers to come to eat. His vision is to demonstrate in a simple and accessible way how to use food to live a life of faith, how to model a life where Jesus is at the centre. Food becomes the connector, a catalyst that makes invitation much easier. Cook describes:

I met a person in a coffee shop that had just moved to the city, invited her for dinner, and in two months she will be baptized and confirmed . . . Two weeks ago, when I was riding in a cab, the taxi driver looked at me and said, 'I've been to your house for dinner. I was homeless then, but I've got myself on me feet now' . . .

The sweetest moment happened when a friend, an accomplished musician who plays for the philharmonic orchestra, grabbed her viola and began to play along with [a man whose life had in many ways been destroyed by alcohol and hard living who had] jumped up to play the piano after dinner.[2]

Somehow the food energizes and brings confidence to those who partake of it, as it should do at every Eucharist shared. Cook continues:

Over the last two and a half years we have had hundreds of people through our doors. We've had people that would never have darkened the door of a church unless someone died or was getting married. And I dare to say, even though I could not have planned it, that some have come and gone, not just with full bellies, but with the sweet taste of Jesus in their mouths; even if they may not have articulated it in such words.[3]

Cook reflects powerfully on the metaphor of 'the table' as a symbol of a 'world put right'. Most depictions of the Last Supper have the disciples, as well as Jesus, sitting at the same level. Here is the idea not just that we all need food to sustain us, millionaire or homeless, black or white, young or old, but also that we need one another through the life and strife of continuous and emerging relationship with others.

The Last Supper is a place of possibility. It is a microcosm of the potential the story of Jesus can have for an often undernourished, wilderness world, for it provides the seedbed for the challenge

Jesus makes through the physical stuff of his own body and his own blood. This meal perpetuates the story of God through one human being's sacrifice, love and new life. For Cook, this is about the table being a place where friends and strangers dream dreams of changing the world, dreams both tiny and ambitious.

Opening up our table is something we can all do; it is not an elite ministry for those 'in the know' – inclusive hospitality, giving body and blood, food and drink, welcome and community. This is Jesus' charge to his disciples, and to us too. The Last Supper is a place where Jesus creates bread, bread in its widest and most mystical of understandings. Bread for absolutely everyone, grace for absolutely everyone, bread for the world is available here. Food can be a means to formulate new futures for ourselves as well as for others.

Prayer and action

- What are your particular 'appetites'? Have you got a healthy attitude to these? If not, what do you need to do?
- Can you remember a time when you were seriously hungry or worried about the provision of food? This Lent, how could you positively use your own hunger to alleviate someone else's? Can you commit to fasting and praying for a community that is suffering from global famine or simply for those with not enough to eat in your own community? Perhaps you could consider giving up one meal each week or going without snacks during Lent. Is there a local food bank you could support?
- Is it appropriate to give up a luxury 'appetite' this Lent and redirect the time, energy or money you might have spent on this to a project that works to alleviate hunger of some kind?
- What does your church community do in terms of fasting? Could you begin a Lent Lunch to bring people together to eat a simple meal and raise awareness of the issue of global and local hunger?
- Reflect on the 'excess' in your life. How might you use this in new ways for the good of others and the glory of God? How might you cut down on your own food waste or other things that are discarded? How might your church community rise to this challenge? Is there a Real Junk Food Café Project or similar near you that you could get involved with? Could you organize a fashion show with second-hand clothes to raise money for charity?
- How does the concept of 'feast' express itself in your life? In the life of your church? Could you introduce something new in terms of a special meal to celebrate or draw others together? Could you initiate a monthly 'feast' event?

- How do you or could you provide 'bread for the world', remembering that this doesn't have to be complicated? How could you take the essence of Ryan Cook's 'open invitation' into your church community in some way? What food event could become a tool for mission for you individually as well as communally? How do you respond to the idea of the table being a 'levelling place'?

WEEK 2

Introduction: identity

As God's children we are deeply loved (1 John 3.1–3)

Identity
A name
Carved on a tree's trunk,
A wooded tattoo.
This name says
I was here,
I have mattered and
I am now (hopefully)
In a different place.
A mark is made on this wooded hill
Where people met and laughed and cried
As at the foot of a cross.
A leaf falls, and one life breaks somewhere
Amidst all eternity.[1]

In a recent episode of BBC Radio 4's *The Public Philosopher*, Michael Sandel discussed the question of how we assimilate an understanding of our identity. Addressing the student audience, he posed the question, 'Do you feel more affinity with the place and people where you grew up or with the environment of your university and your fellow students?' Behind this question lay an invitation to deeper reflection: where do we locate the factors that make up our personhood? Is it the town where we grew up, our class, our sexuality, our faith, our interests or our intellectual level?

All of us are a melting-pot mixture of personal history, built and honed by places, experiences and individuals that have had an impact on our lives thus far. Interesting questions to ask ourselves are, 'If someone were to ask you to describe yourself in one sentence, what is the first thing you would say? How would you define the essence of who you are?'

As human beings, all of us have intrinsic value; as Christians, we believe every person who has ever lived is loved by a God of love, regardless of physical make-up, demographics or financial accumulation. We have daily choices to make in terms of how we respond to the world, and faith in Christ tells us we can be redeemed, remade, enabled to live as new creations every day.

The passage from 1 John tells the early Christians that their primary identity comes from a knowledge that they are, as we are, children of God. We are loved by him and, as history unfolds, we are moving gradually into a fuller understanding of who Christ is, for we are called to be like him. The purpose of John's letter is to recalibrate followers to reject the false teaching that is telling them that evil results from an encounter with the physical world and that Christ, as God's Son, could not have been a human being. Psalm 139.14 tells its readers that they are 'fearfully and wonderfully made' – precious as individuals – but what makes us complete is an identity bound up with this God of pure and unadulterated love.

Who we are and how we navigate ourselves in the world can feel like a wilderness experience in our time. We learn the rules of our society and culture in order to survive as well as thrive. Our challenge as Christians is to reflect on how we approach the world and the impact we have on it and on others who live in it. Our individuality makes the world colourful as each of us brings our culture, our dress sense, our personality, our sense of humour, our perspective on the world into every relationship that we make, fleeting or sustained. We are given the gift of uniquely being able to inhabit *one* life and to live it from this singular perspective.

In this chapter we will move through a trajectory to explore what happens when this individuality takes us further away from others as it resides in solitude or loneliness. The isolation Jesus experiences in Gethsemane, ironically surrounded by his closest friends, is acute and wrapped up in his unusual and costly calling. But the 40-day wilderness is a strange refreshment, a girding of inner strength to confront his individual calling to be both Son of Man as well as Son of God. To be free to live alone well is one of the greatest challenges for us in the West, in a forum saturated with the making of 'connections', which ironically often push us away from substantial and safe flesh-and-blood encounters with others. Loneliness is one of the tragedies of our age, where many hearts ache for the substantial and sustainable company of others.

Most of us connect our identities with our family and friends. Friendship, for a reason, a season or a lifetime is something that sustains us in moments of pain as well as enabling us to celebrate life in its most resplendent moments. Jesus models this well with the disciples as he chooses a miscellany of close friends from all walks of life and social strata. Friendship at its best is a grace-filled experience, and there is something deeply spiritual about good friendship as it listens, soothes, challenges and supports us when life feels rough. Jesus moves from calling his disciples 'servants' to calling them 'friends' as he approaches his final hours.

Our identity also sites us automatically in a variety of small and larger communities. As people who follow Jesus, we are challenged to draw others into our community of faith, however we understand this, especially those who are lonely and vulnerable, and to exhibit openness and welcome. In his book *Being Human*, Rowan Williams observes that, as individuals who inhabit bodies, we cannot make sense of the world without interacting with others. We work out our lives in relation to others: 'I cannot invent language for myself: I have to be spoken *to*. I cannot picture myself as a body or a self unless I am seen and engaged *with*.'[2] He continues that such connection involves three things: *attention*, *attunement* and *atonement*. In other words, in every situation where we have an impact on others, we have the extraordinary capacity to give others our attention, to negotiate that attention as we adjust to our encounters and, finally, we carry the capacity to be 'at one' with each person or situation.

This dynamic is simply how we live as we negotiate ourselves as individuals every time we encounter another. It is an indication that we not only need to find approaches to living in community that are meaningful and harmonious for ourselves but, as people who carry distinctive faith, we can also model something for the world. We ask the questions: What are the communities in which we reside? What kinds of communities do we want to live in, and when we create these, how does faith make a difference?

The poem that begins this chapter describes the human experience of carving a **name** on a tree, setting an individual **identity** within a more expansive and perhaps eternal natural order. It explores how vital it is within our humanity to understand that, as Christians, we need to be at home within the **solitude** of our own existence as well as search out those who feel lost and isolated, along with others who live continually in a hidden but anguished **loneliness**. The Passion Narrative reminds us that Jesus went to the cross for love and love alone, and he calls those who are his followers to use the energy of this to move beyond the healthy and happy **relationships and friendships**, given to us as gift, to create **community** where potentially all God's children can experience the fact that we are precious. Located as people in our own right as well as people who live together with others, we know that all of us, in some way, need to leave a legacy, to make our mark, and that our names are etched on the heart of God and were etched on the cross of Christ.

Name

God promises to rescue his people and tells them they are called by name (Isaiah 43.1–4)

A recent news article reported the death of the oldest spider in the world, a female known as 'Number 16', at the age of 43. Scientists were devastated at the demise of this trapdoor arachnid, having had high hopes that she would reach the grand old age of 50. It was a shame that a spider with such a claim to fame had been relegated to a number rather than designated with a proper name, but perhaps if she had, the scientists observing her on a daily basis would have needed bereavement counselling![1]

Names tell us about who we are, often indicating cultural or socio-economic background and sometimes religious faith. Our names give us a dignity which locates us in the world and enables us to have a place within it, regardless of our achievements and failures. Even if we don't like our names, few of us take the trouble to change them; they are so integral to our identity and history that we find them difficult to dispense with easily.

Our names often hold meaning – we might have been named for a reason, after another member of our family or a place that is special to our parents. My own name holds some significance for both my parents as well as for me. I was born after the day when Mary Magdalene is celebrated in the Anglican lectionary, the nearest female saint to my birthday. And the character of Magdalene is also deeply meaningful to me as my own vocation has emerged and developed. Magdalene is the first person who sees the risen Christ in each of the four Gospels. In John, she recognizes Christ when he calls her by her name – that is all that is needed for her to understand that he is alive once again. Once over the shock, she is commanded to go and tell the other disciples, and presumably had to muster up the courage to do so. In the years before synod's decision to ordain women as priests, and as I entered the discernment process feeling called to priestly ministry, there was initially no clear indication that I would be able to exercise such a ministry in an authorized capacity.

The words of Isaiah 43 are familiar to many of us, with their spirit of grace-filled consolation, speaking of a God who knows each person, and of how we are called into his world through his love. We are redeemed and precious in his sight and he promises to share our journey through life, whatever it may bring. A name gathers the irreducible mystery of who someone is into one being, a being who is utterly unique. Within one name is a whole world of history, culture, experience, narrative and belief.

In the Bible, names are significant. Protagonists are *renamed*, often after significant spiritual awakenings or after momentous events. Abram, 'esteemed father', becomes Abraham, meaning 'father of a multitude'. Sarai becomes Sarah – 'mother of nations'. Their names are symbolic of their significance as the Father and Mother of the state of Israel, God's chosen people. In the New Testament, Saul is renamed as Paul once his conversion and growth in faith have been established. Such renaming signifies the start of a new adventure.

But names can also send shivers down spines because of past associations as well as branding people for ever because of history. Names can take us back to times of wilderness and terror. During periods of history when people have ceased to be named and have instead been relegated to numbers, then the slippery slope to dehumanization has begun. This is why slavery, genocide and the Holocaust remain rightly so utterly abhorrent to our innate sense of humanity and preciousness, the sense that every human person has something of grace within them, that every person reflects something of the divine and thus their personhood is sacred. In the Passion Narrative, the names of Pilate and Judas have become historical *bêtes noires*, entrenched symbols of weakness and betrayal, however unfairly.

But whether positive or negative, our names matter, which is why, when we meet a stranger, it is interesting to reflect on the moment when we ask them their name, if indeed we do. That moment signifies a great deal. It is a tentative searching out of a new level of relationship, a request to enter another's life with a yearning to make a connection, even if only for a short time. Knowing someone's name plants the seeds of friendship. It grounds conversations in a different way and deanonymizes the other. The asking or giving of a person's name means that we view that person as someone who matters, with opinions, feelings and experiences that have value and that make that person who he or she is.

The asking or giving of someone's name is an invitation into a level of intimacy and is when we begin to stand on holy ground. Potentially, a life unfolds. Knowing and remembering a person's name come less easily for many of us as we move through life accumulating more friends and acquaintances. But when we do, people are sometimes surprised and often delighted that we have remembered who they are; they somehow feel that they matter and that something of their life has been imprinted on our own as a connection is re-established.

Jesus' name communicates a multitude of complex messages throughout the Gospels. The crowds at their most mesmerized and adoring whisper the name of Jesus as someone they want to follow, someone who promises a way to freedom from oppression. Jesus questions his own disciples, asking, 'Who do people say that I am?' (Mark 8.27), but as he does so he rejects the names of former prophets as reference points. Standing before Pilate, Jesus ceases to be named and is instead anonymized. His identity and actions are labelled as blasphemous in order for his arrest to be easier. But as he hangs on the cross, his personhood runs alongside his title: 'Jesus of Nazareth, the King of the Jews'.

The cross is not a bad place to finish, for it draws together profoundly in wood and in flesh the vertical 'I' of our own individuality, Christian identity and vocation, whatever that may be – the delight God has in each human being. But the horizontal beam of the cross creates a 'T': the 'T' of togetherness, of relationship and community, the fact that no individual can find true meaning or purpose unless their life is lived alongside others. It was not one person who brought Jesus to his death, but a whole community, hypnotized by false values and easy options. But equally it was individuals, renamed and revitalized, that established the Church: Peter and Paul. One person, iconic in name – be it Mandela, Malala or Magdalene – leads people out and away from their basest and most unbelieving levels towards a new vision of a world redeemed.

Loneliness

Gethsemane
(Mark 14.32–42)

Loneliness is hallmarked by an intense desire to bring the experience to a close; something which cannot be achieved by sheer willpower or by simply getting out more, but only by developing intimate connections. This is far easier said than done, especially for people whose loneliness arises from a state of loss or exile or prejudice, who have reason to fear or mistrust as well as long for the society of others.

. . . the lonelier a person gets, the less adept they become at navigating social currents. Loneliness grows around them, like mould or fur, a prophylactic that inhibits contact, no matter how badly contact is desired.

(Olivia Laing, *The Lonely City*, quoted in *Eleanor Oliphant Is Completely Fine* by Gail Honeyman)[1]

Jesus is bone-cold alone. The breeze of a Mediterranean night makes no difference to his chilled soul. At no other point in the Gospels do we read of the strength of his feelings so acutely, with verse 33 saying, 'He took with him Peter and James and John, and began to be distressed.' The Good News Bible renders Jesus' words as, 'The sorrow in my heart is so great that it almost crushes me.' The disciples are commanded to, at the very least, stay with him and keep watch. But they cannot even do this, as one by one they fall asleep.

Jesus is alone, even though he is surrounded by his closest friends, who do not, cannot, share the loneliness and spiritual torment he is experiencing. This is the point in his life when the reality that he has embarked on a pathway that has inevitable consequences is grasped by him and others, for it is a pathway that will lead to the end of his earthly life, a spectacular reversal of the popularity he enjoyed in his brief years of teaching and preaching. I imagine Jesus crouching by a rock in Gethsemane, perhaps observing casual visitors passing through the garden on a balmy night, who stroll nonchalantly after a good meal, oblivious of the fate that awaits him.

Mark's Gospel uses vivid language. Jesus throws himself on the ground, praying fervently that this cup of suffering – a violent death which he must know to be a possibility – be taken from him. He wants desperately to live a different life. Having preached that faith can move mountains, he now wants a miracle to happen for *him*; he wants the nightmare to end, to walk away from this ordeal. Jesus desperately tries to rouse his friends, to maintain their company, even if it is a weak fellowship, but it is no use.

Gethsemane reminds us that Jesus goes through a deep loneliness in that place, and that discipleship has a similar cost for all who choose to genuinely follow him, because we too are asked to enter the experience of his life. Jesus has become, at this point, a social outcast, a scapegoat, a freak, a person to be dispensed with. What happens to him has resonances with all who are on the edge of popularity, even on the edge of survival, and who show us something of what it might mean to share in the solidarity of a Christlike existence.

Loneliness comes in many forms. It can be chosen as well as imposed. Loneliness often happens when a person is, ironically, surrounded by others. It often leads to isolation, which means a state of separation among individuals or groups as well as a feeling of being disliked and alone. As our society changes the nature of how it presents and creates community, a variety of people, often vulnerable, fall through the net to become prisoners of loneliness in a world obsessed with having friends, constant communication and with at least the appearance of being popular.

The Christian gospel has always resulted in individuals and groups being 'set apart', creating communities that go against the flow of a culture of often conflicting values to the ones Jesus advocated. But such a community asks those who belong to it to reach out to the world and to remain in the world through love. Its message is to take special responsibility to notice, name and include those who sometimes so suddenly find themselves without security and company as they teeter on the precipice of emotional and physical survival. Even when individuals are not physically vulnerable, being liked and respected can change in a lightning strike, societal pressure and opinion devouring its victims as they struggle to maintain the truth in any one situation.

The Florida Project is a potent indie film, directed by Sean Baker. The film is seen through the eyes of six-year-old Moonee, an ebullient wild child who lives in a budget hotel on the edge of Orlando's Disney World. The Magic Castle motel is for social misfits abandoned by a world promoting the American dream, whose proponents would much rather pretend it didn't exist.

A far cry from Disney's fantasies, it's a place where mattresses are infested with bedbugs, and stray paedophiles prey on the residents' kids. Its psychedelic purple walls mask the loneliness, poverty and isolation that Halley, Moonee's defiant and dysfunctional single mother, lives with daily. Halley behaves atrociously throughout the film, and we watch her in her roles of mother, friend and motel resident as her raw and tragic life unfolds. She hawks perfume, works as a prostitute, swears, steals and eats her way through a fast-food life in the grim squalor of a single room which is the home where she is bringing up her daughter. Isolated already because of her upbringing, class, lifestyle and general desperation, the film shows the decisive spiralling down which isolates her even further, making her unpopular and on the edge of even this heartsick community.

The faithful and long-suffering motel manager, Bobby, does his best to make sure Halley stays on the right side of the law, which she does until the very end, by the skin of her teeth. Already isolated herself, probably as a result of bad parenting, Halley is essentially a lost child, and she plays this out through a calamitous as well as joyful approach to her life which feels challenging to watch.

Jesus' challenge to those who wish to listen is always anti-isolationist. In Gethsemane he pleads that his disciples 'keep awake' to remain aware of his plight, to be alongside him in his hard waiting. In the Gospels he reaches out to individuals and groups who believe themselves to be superior, to those who believe themselves to be holier, to those who are disliked and vilified because of their social status, sex, profession or past, effectively to say, 'Stop the isolation, step out from your darkness, take my hand and join the dance to enter the alternative reality of God's kingdom.'

The Jesus scholar Marcus Borg comments:

> Community is utterly central to Christianity, as it is to all enduring religions. Community of praise, community of nourishment . . . the most nourishing thing I can do for my Christian journey is to be part of a worshipping community that sings its heart out.[2]

Community is also about the process of formation, a place where resocialization into a new identity and way of being can happen to anyone willing to participate. This, Borg states, is about a decisive stance against the values of an American (and western) way of life which, with its obsession with the three As of appearance, affluence and achievement, has become so radically different from anything that is recognizably Christian.[3] Transforming loneliness into community through grace must go way beyond simply handing out food parcels from the back of a van, which is done at the Magic Castle motel by well-meaning Christian groups. It's about understanding why people have been shunted into forgotten places as well as believing that community can happen here too, and offering a new friendship in a new language in which hope can be heard afresh.

Solitude

Jesus reflects on his singular status as God's Son (John 16.31–33)

I didn't seek solitude, it sought me. It evolved gradually after my marriage broke down. I found myself living on my own in a small country village. At first, I was miserable and cross. It took between six months and a year before I noticed that I had become phenomenally happy.
(Sara Maitland, British writer and solitary)[1]

Most of us are only a very short distance from being alone, says Andrew Haigh, exploring the theme of solitude in his recent film *Lean on Pete* in an interview on BBC Radio 4. He is right: aloneness can come upon us at a moment's notice, through bereavement, poverty or the sudden decline of our physical and mental faculties, as it does to his young protagonist, Charlie, who loses his single-parent father when he is shot dead in front of him.

In an age of self-sufficiency, most of us are essentially vulnerable in this sense, and the onslaught of social media, as well as the pressure to be among people constantly, keeps us from facing the fact that we entered and will leave this life essentially alone. Sara Maitland, the writer and Christian solitary, talks in the above quote about solitude finding her rather than the other way around. She differentiates between solitude being the fact and loneliness being a negative response to this experience.

The solitary life is one that removes a person decisively, sometimes defiantly, to plumb the depths of the divine. The first Christian hermits were those who positioned themselves in the Egyptian and Syrian deserts in the fourth and fifth centuries in order to face the fallenness of their own naked humanity and the depravity of the world, and via these to move through their own loneliness to reconnect with a living God who is present in every person. Their recorded experience of discipline and facing demons is a far cry from narcissistic and unadulterated introspection and far more a release of heart, mind and soul for God alone. Their experience told them that in order to understand how to truly love others and to understand their own place in the world they were called to face themselves with rigorous honesty, a journey of learning gradually to be at peace on their own. The Carmelite vow takes up Abbot Moses' famous challenge: 'Go sit in your cell and your cell will teach you everything.'[2]

The Celtic saints similarly carry a reputation for living their Christian mission primarily alone. St Ninian, in the south west of Scotland, spent much of his life in a cave overlooking the sea. But from this experience grew an expansive sense of love and service for others, and legend tells that many people sought Ninian out to heal and provide wisdom.

More recently there has been an emerging interest in the eremitic life, and contemporary hermits have been attracted to the silence of the wild and weathered natural world through living immersed in the elements, as Verena Schiller describes so exquisitely in her book, *A Simplified Life*,[3] about her time as a hermit on the Llŷn Peninsula, North Wales. Christian solitaries usually feel a strong compulsion to pray, and to pray a great deal, so that their lives become in tune with the heartbeat of a loving God.

Most of us are not called to live in a cave or even in a mobile caravan on the edge of a cliff, but to understand being alone as a positive experience is an emotional as well as a spiritual resource. Sara Maitland comments, 'I feel we haven't created space for children to find out what they need. I've never heard of being sent to your room as a reward.'[4] Solitude is about us being at peace with our essential selves, not feeling threatened or incomplete by being alone, even though solitude might feel enabled because we know that in the background of our lives there are others who love and support us and whose own lives would feel impoverished without us.

Jesus needs time and space to be alone as well. The Gospel accounts record that he regularly withdraws to be alone, to fill himself once more with God's power after the demands of healing and prophecy. Luke 5.16 has this happening after Jesus has called the first disciples and after he has healed a man with leprosy. The text records specifically that this is a lonely place, a place where Jesus would encounter no one else. After numerous healings, Mark 1.35 has Jesus rising early to go again to a solitary place to pray, even though Simon and the other disciples quickly search him out. Luke 6.12 has Jesus taking himself away after the grumblings of the Pharisees and teachers of the law, who witnessed him exploding the religious practices of the Sabbath. Jesus tells his disciples in John 16 that the time is coming when they too will be left alone because he is going to his Father.

Deep peace comes when and if we can be brave enough to explore the essential and integral loneliness of life, when we accept that our lives can be precarious and unpredictable, and also that being alone can be restorative and an aid to deepening an understanding of what we are about. Through life this ability fluctuates – there are times when we run towards aloneness while at others it feels like an open wound.

I was struck a few weeks ago by an observation I made while swimming one morning in my local pool. As I began swimming my regular lengths, I noticed a middle-aged woman waiting at one end. She had already spoken to me in the changing room and was now beginning a conversation with another swimmer. The conversation continued for a good 10–15 minutes as I carried on swimming. After the second woman indicated that she must do her own swimming, the woman also began to swim. But she swam only two lengths and then stepped out of the pool. She had swum three lengths in total.

I concluded that this woman was lonely and was using the public nature of the pool to seek out another human being simply to speak to. But many go to the pool, as I did on that occasion, happy to depart from the busyness and noise of life, happy to be alone yet surrounded by others.

Individuals who are essentially happy to reside in a state of solitude become something of a countercultural symbol, one that sometimes challenges those who cannot, for whatever reason, face being alone. Being alone can drift into an agonizing loneliness when this is unwanted, but perhaps we are challenged to also exhibit a happy stability in the state of our own solitariness, to communicate that we are not afraid to face the reality of who we are. Hermits and mystics through the ages, by living solitary lives also live simplified lives, lives where the landscape and natural world are listened to with acute awareness as they travel into a deeper and more numinous rhythm that speaks to us amid myriad distractions.

Solitude is far from a negative state or a symbol of a failed existence; it can become the perceiving of divine presence in the present moment and in the changing seasons of our lives as it cleanses, refines and enriches our souls.

Friendship

Jesus' new commandment to his disciples (John 15.15–17)

Friendship is no passing feeling of affection. It combines affection with faithfulness. Between friends there rules only the promise to walk with each other and to be there for each other, a faithfulness that has to do not with acting and possessing but with the individual person and with being.
(Jürgen Moltmann, *The Open Church*)[1]

If these are the dynamics of human friendship, they may also be a clue to friendship with God.
(James Nelson, *The Intimate Connection*)[2]

In his lengthy soliloquy in John 15, Jesus begins to prepare his disciples for his last days. He talks about connection, a new community, which can be formed like the metaphorical vine – a healthy plant with branches growing and supporting one another. Then he talks about love, but a love that is like no other. Love, not as a romcom optional extra, but as a *commandment*, an active verb for which there is no alternative but to put it into practice.

To his often doltish disciples Jesus spells it out: they are no longer to understand themselves as servants (if there was any doubt before) but as *friends*. Friends, because friends are trusted with important, often confidential, information – at this time, precious pearls of wisdom which are to form the basis of the new vision God has for the world. They are friends because 'I have made known to you everything that I have heard from my Father' (John 15.15).

47

Moreover, their selection *as* friends is a decisive choosing by Jesus, even though most of the time they don't fully understand why. But the truth remains: they have become not just the guardians but also the conduits through which the kingdom will be promoted and established with the work of God's phenomenal Spirit.

Perhaps Jesus is anticipating the loneliness of the final stage of his journey and this is why his words feel especially dramatic. Human as he is, he knows he will have to walk this part of his life alone. Certain occasions in our own lives require us to do the same, however 'not alone' we are. No one can feel what we feel as we experience bereavement, serious illness or a yearning to have something we don't yet have or to be somewhere we haven't yet got to. These times can be wilderness experiences, often of intensity and magnitude. But to know at least that we have others alongside us, even as a presence, somehow can help ease that trudge through the chilly coldness of a dark-tunnel time. Every human being needs others, even those who are introverted, those who prefer their own company, and those who are bad tempered most of the time.

John Donne and Thomas Merton were right that no person is or can be an island. We are all dependent in some way upon others, even if our relationship with them is ambiguous. Most of us, however weird or antisocial, have at least one or two people we feel connected to and can describe as friends.

Friendship comes in many forms. We can be friendly people who have the ability to get talking to anyone, wherever we find ourselves hanging out. Our social communities might amount to a wide circle of friends, smaller groups where deeper and more sustaining relationships are built, or hundreds of 'friends' on Facebook or other social platforms, but all this depends on our personalities, our contexts and our lifestyles.

To cultivate the ability to 'be friendly', to be sensed as a person who carries around an aura of welcome, is perhaps a quality most Christians can at least attempt to aspire to. More than anything it helps the world to feel a gentler, more hopeful place when there is so much desolation and loneliness. Being friendly, far from sounding trite, can provide life-giving emotional support and witness extra-ordinary results.

Gareth, also a priest, tells the moving story of a relationship he established with a recovering alcoholic. Daniel walked into his church, following one of the steps of Alcoholics Anonymous which encourages participants to 'believe that a Power greater than ourselves can restore us to sanity'. Gareth, through general welcome and being at least a clerical 'friend', got to know Daniel through his attendance at services in his church.

However, after being dry for two years, Daniel resumed drinking heavily after splitting up with his girlfriend. A few months later, as Gareth was praying, he was suddenly overcome with the urge to go and visit this man. As he was walking to Daniel's home, he met him as Daniel was going to the supermarket to buy yet another bottle of gin. As he encountered Gareth, Daniel was overwhelmed by this priest's concern for his well-being and in his simply being there as a faithful friend. For Daniel, this was a 'God-incidence' of the person who represented divine help and care appearing in his life again, and they returned to Daniel's flat, which was in a state of disarray, dirty clothes and crockery, and general chaos.

The visit from Gareth made Daniel decide to give up alcohol again as well as to ask for the job he had lost because of it, a few months earlier. For Gareth, this was merely the arm of simple, Spirit-inspired friendship – of listening to the call and yearning for a God who seeks for every person to be loved, to be in relationship with others.[3]

The hit sitcom *Friends*, which aired from 1994 to 2004, remains one of the most popular television programmes ever. It has as part of its catchy theme tune the phrase, 'I'll be there for you.' This is essentially the bottom line of all friendships, and is the dynamic described above in the relationship between Graham and Daniel. Indeed, when our friends aren't there for us, we feel a shattering sense of upset and disloyalty. In the words of Nell Goddard, *Friends* is 'a classic mix of things that are good and true and beautiful – friendship, loyalty, honesty – and things which are twisted and broken – casual sex, selfishness, and jealousy. That's part of what makes it so relatable.'4

Perhaps it seems strange that such a series remained so popular, a simple sitcom based around only six friends where no real plot develops except the interpersonal relationships of the characters themselves. But this is also the stuff of life, where a group of friends becomes the human melting pot where those included have the chance to either become great or remain small and meagre.

How we interact with others and how we choose to love them will form us as well as provide a witness to how we respond in a multitude of ways. As the Passion Narrative unfolds, it is the same for the disciples, who through friendship experience the rise and fall of that classic mix of loyalty and nonchalant weakness that all of us in our capacity as 'friend' have displayed at one point or other, from the weak betrayal of Peter by the courtyard fire to the resilient steadfastness of the women at the foot of the cross. Friendship is built from relationship and has the capacity to transform a life.

Community

What a Christian community looks like (Philippians 2.1–8)

Love is neither sentimental nor a passing emotion. It is an attraction to others which gradually becomes commitment, the recognition of a covenant of a mutual belonging. (Jean Vanier, 1928–2019)[1]

Jean Vanier describes the concept of community in far from idyllic terms:

A community isn't just a place where people live under the same roof; that is a lodging house or an hotel. Nor is a community a work-team. It is a place where everyone is emerging from the shadows of egocentricity to the light of real love. It is the space where most members are making the transition, caught up perhaps in something mysteriously powerful, which is moving them slowly but surely away from 'the community of myself' into a changed dynamic travelling to become 'myself for the community'.[2]

Today we live, for the most part, surrounded by people. We live as part of both healthy and dysfunctional communities. Many of us feel attracted to the ideal of community; it is a natural human yearning – to create links with others who share a common interest, world view, lifestyle. Community can be our own family, the geographical place where we physically reside, our faith or interest group, or a way of belonging that is more dispersed. We flow in and out of various communities as we move through our lives, and often the imprint of those we have encountered and the experience of belonging, acceptance or rejection remains.

In Philippians 2, Paul describes to the people of Philippi his own understanding of this. At the heart of any community must be the person of Christ. The Holy Spirit inspires friendship and encourages unselfish and expansive attitudes towards one another – compassion, kindness, humility and patience. Members of a strong and good community look out for one another's interests, not just their own. Grounded always in the nature of Christ, we see this as a movement from egoism to service, from a dying of self to the reforming of self in the light of understanding and loving others.

Community is therefore not a cosy or comfortable banning of insecurity; it does not provide an escape from the pressures or anxieties of the current world, but rather it provides a purifying fire where we learn to trust in the delightful individuality of one another while working amid the craggy idiosyncrasies, the deepest annoyances and the most magnanimous kindnesses we are each capable of, clothed in the power of God. Vanier describes this as 'the passing from a land of slavery to a promised land, the land of interior freedom'.[3]

Jesus' own metaphors for living together are community-centric: the vine and its branches that can bear fruit but also need pruning, the field with both wheat and tares where each grows alongside the other, the sheep and the goats, the disciples themselves in all their imperfect and broken variety. Community is simultaneously beautiful, a potential antidote to loneliness, and a place where we come face to face with ourselves through interaction with others.

It has been and is often said that community is a hard place to truly live, for it asks of us the setting aside of our own agendas for the good of the whole, an acceptance that all members are of equal importance whatever they may or may not contribute. When we live closely with others in any 'community', it can be hard not to know everything that is wrong with one another, including all our complicated stories and messy mistakes. This brings choice: we can either remain in judgement of those we live with, or we can decisively embrace others in the knowledge that God's love desires always to move us onwards into a more generous relationship with those we find challenging.

Good community provides the catalyst for its members to cease to stagnate spiritually and contains the potential for the deepening of an understanding of love as well as opportunities for conversion. Yet community can be a wilderness place too, a place where we need time to gain the sense of belonging, time to absorb the commonalities, the shared faith or purpose of the whole. Community can be a lonely place where we feel out of kilter, our own world and ways of interpreting it clashing with the understood and accepted norms.

Call the Midwife has become one of the nation's favourite programmes for Sunday evening viewing. The year 2019 saw its eighth series as the story continued around the hub that is Nonnatus House, a genuine historical place (St Frideswide's Mission House), where a community of nuns (from the Community of St John the Divine) and midwives eat, live and pray together as they go about their daily work of serving the area of Poplar, East London, itself a rainbow community of poor, diverse, settled and immigrant people. Both nuns and midwives bring their issues, which are familiar to us in the twenty-first century: alcoholism, the prejudice faced as a gay person or an ethnic minority, mental fragility and the demands of a vocational job that ask for a response at every hour of the day. Over the years the series has been running, most life issues have been washed, rinsed and spun in the laundry of this community house.

But here is no straightforward or twee harking back to a 1960s golden age where sumptuous high teas were calmly eaten and manners were exemplary. Here are imperturbable and mettlesome women, brave enough to face not only the complexities of giving birth in often difficult circumstances but also the gritty reality of some of the healthcare challenges of the period: illegal abortions, thalidomide children, injuries at work well before Health and Safety regulations came into being. What might be described as 'holy commentary' floats over each episode at the beginning and end of the programme, the offering of gentle wisdom, often with a deeply Christian strand, which centres on the redemptive power of living alongside one another in a grace-filled and genuine community. Here community is modelled as holding a genuinely redemptive power, where the small irritations as well as life's big issues are gently held as well as worked through as the members of this community become beacons of light and hope for the wider urban community in which they serve.

Prayer and action

- Reflect on where you find your own identity. What factors make you who you are before God at this present time?
- Does your own name have any significance to you? What does it say about you and what might God be calling you into through the gift of it? Otherwise, perhaps there are people close to you whose names do hold significance. Can you use this as a basis for a discussion or prayer focus in a home or study group?
- Who are the people you know who live in a state of solitude daily? Can you identify those who feel content and at peace with this and those who are lonely? What can you learn from both sets of people and how do you respond to them? Can your church provide a forum where this can be talked about openly? How could you or your church help those who are significantly challenged by loneliness? Do you yourself feel lonely?
- Can you identify those who are isolated in your community? What are the factors that create this situation? Where are the places and who are the people who offer some solace in such isolation? Can the church or other organizations help?
- Who have been your most important friends over the years? What is it about them that makes friendship work? Reflect on which friends you have had for a reason, a season or a lifetime. How can you provide friendship to someone new in your place of work, church or community?
- Pray for those people with few friends or who are at odds with their friends.

- Where are the communities you inhabit? What are the life-giving components of these? What are the things that drain these of life? Can you discuss which dynamics create a healthy community in a study or home group?
- Do the boundaries of the communities you inhabit need stretching to become more hospitable or inclusive?

WEEK 3

Introduction: occupation

Jesus prays for his own vocation and the continuation of this by his disciples (John 17)

The lavender bush
A fragrant purple sphere,
A blooming contribution for perfect bee-ing.
Mauve and muggy scent
in this summer of relentless and determined heat.
Occupied territory
Of busy ingenuity
Amongst its delicate pinnacles.
Bees use and abuse its nectar as refugees have to do;
A Martha-and-Mary bush,
A vocation to be beautiful and useful, it gives its musky love to
All that which passes through.[1]

In an era of busyness and time poverty, how do people of faith approach the time that is given to us? Lent begins with Jesus taking time to spend 40 days of emptiness to contemplate what will be a busy and demanding ministry. Ecclesiastes 3 famously tells readers that there is an appropriate time for everything. In much of life today it can feel as though we do all of the things it mentions in 24 hours, never mind in distinctive seasons.

'Occupation' can be suggestive of the job we do, a specific career path we have trained for, or, more broadly, the word asks, 'How do we occupy ourselves?' How we fill our days can feel deeply satisfying and meaningful as we work at a job we love, the satisfaction and nurturing of a family, and myriad other things. Or our days can feel full of wilderness, bleak and never-ending as we do not have those things in place, and talk is of third-generation unemployment and how to 'kill time'. In our society we often take an unspoken moral high ground as we judge others in terms of how they occupy their time, and often put greater importance on career paths that earn large amounts of money or sound glamorous.

John 17 has Jesus giving to God his three intensive years of ministry. He feels he has come to the end of his own mission. Jesus recognizes that he has been given authority to do what he has done in God's power, all for the glory of his Father. He has imparted a vision of a new way of living and of spending time. Even if he has not been entirely successful in this vision, he believes he has come to the end of his own work, as he says in verse 4 of John 17, 'I glorified you on earth by finishing the work that you gave me to do.'

In his ministry, Jesus challenges good and bad work: Zacchaeus the manipulator of taxes, the overturning of the tables in the temple when sacred space is not being occupied correctly, the parable of the talents which encourages the positive use of time and money, and the affirmation of the practical Martha as well as the more contemplative Mary. Inherent in the above verses from John is a deep sense that everything we do and are involved in shines with divine life and that all we have is a gift which is given to us from God.

There is liberation in this. Embedded in the Christian tradition is the idea that, however we occupy our days, all is within the presence of God and should be done for his glory to the best of our ability. This idea is powerfully translatable at whatever stage of life we are at – whether we have a busy career or are taking time to nurture a family at home or are filling our latter days with meaning and purpose. To approach the time we have responsibly and for the service of others is tantamount to a life lived in Christ.

The German mystic, Meister Eckhart, says:

In this regard, one kind of work does indeed differ from another but if one takes the same attitude toward each of his various occupations, then they will be all alike to him. Thus being on the right track and God meaning this to him, he will shine, as clear in worldly things as heavenly.[2]

The seventeenth-century French Archbishop François de la Fénelon offers a challenge about the use of time, which feels strangely contemporary:

> Thus let us spend our days, redeeming the time, by quitting vain amusements, useless correspondence, those weak outpourings of the heart that are only modifications of self-love, and conversations that dissipate the mind, and lead to no good. Thus, shall we find time to serve God; and there is none well employed that is not devoted to him.[3]

Questionable, therefore, is the gossip I involve myself in, the celebrity magazines I read, the useless television I watch and the endless hours on Facebook I spend.

This chapter explores how we **occupy** our time and our attitude towards work and career, and reflects on how faith could have an impact upon these more powerfully. There are various stories of **ambition** in the Bible, of how, rightly channelled and executed, it helps us to grow into our potential and reach for the stars. Wrongly inhabited, it insidiously undermines all that we are and can be for God's glory and makes us bitter, jealous and deeply unsatisfied with who we are and what we have.

Position explores a faith-based and healthy way of inhabiting leadership. **Vocation** is a decisive approach to whatever we do, a deep sense that whatever it is we are involved in, it is something we are compelled to do that is Spirit-led. Vocation explores how discovering our gifts and talents meets the needs of the world as we walk with God to offer these in loving service. We reflect on the idea of **contribution** – what happens when people give even a little (which is often a great deal) and how powerful this can be. It is interesting that in the revised criteria for selection for ordained ministry the word **service** has reappeared more definitively, a reminder that in an increasingly individually focused society even the Church must not lose sight of its gentle insistence that to be a Christian disciple is about a sense of service to God and to others.

The poem at the beginning of this chapter describes a simple lavender bush, how it contributes to a garden simply by its presence. Its own vocation is to grow and flourish, just as itself, to be beautiful, yet it also contributes by providing nourishment for the bees and insects that pass through its stems. A horticultural Martha as well as Mary, it is both ontological and functional, a metaphor for the utmost of human flourishing.

How we ourselves occupy our work, our time, our faith and the changing nature of life itself is a Lenten and continuous question which can take us into the wilderness as well as bring us seasons of radiant grace.

Ambition

James and John have a special request (Mark 10.35–45)

There's something nesting here, something horrible waiting.
Ambition, Rose. It squeezes us into corners and turns out ugly
shapes.
(Tim Winton, *Cloudstreet*)[1]

Ambition has its etymological root from the Latin *ambitio* or *ambitus*, meaning 'going around, circuit, edge or border'. Initially this referred to the collecting of votes during the early Roman republic as a means of canvassing for various political positions. Over time, however, the word began to take on other connotations, including to refer to those ambitious individuals who would stop at nothing to gain honour, popularity and power. Psychologists such as Abraham Maslow in the 1940s contextualized ambition in terms of a 'hierarchy of needs', arguing that within one humanity we carry different needs and motivations which compete with one another.

In our schools, further educational establishments and many career sectors, ambition has become a quality to aspire to, yet ambition in church circles proves to be something of a dirty word. It is a concept we talk about in hushed whispers, usually about someone else, with implications that to be ambitious as a Christian person (particularly as an ordained person) is not quite right, that it betrays the idea of servant-hearted ministry and recollects past eras where being ordained equalled power, position and wealth. Yet the Church, as one bishop described to me, is notoriously flat: there are relatively few senior posts compared to the number of highly intelligent and capable people who are within it. Perhaps this is also true of other occupations, although in these it feels somehow easier, and more honest, to be able to state that we have some kind of idea of where we want to get to within a chosen profession or role.

Ambition itself is not a bad thing, for it suggests we want to be stretched to use our God-given gifts to their maximum potential. It is about a deep yearning for us to somehow 'make our mark'. Anthony Ashley Cooper, Seventh Earl of Shaftesbury in the nineteenth century, says, 'Time was when I could not sleep for ambition. I thought of nothing but fame and immortality. I could not bear the idea of dying and being forgotten.'[2]

A famous piece of writing by Marianne Williamson describes the more human reticence to engage with ambition:

> It is our light not our darkness that most frightens us. We ask ourselves, who am I to be brilliant, gorgeous, talented, fabulous? Actually, who are you not to be? You are a child of God. Your playing small does not serve the world. There is nothing enlightened about shrinking so that other people won't feel insecure around you . . . We were born to make manifest the glory of God that is within us.[3]

The parable of the labourers in the vineyard is all about this – using the gifts and talents given to us to expand a larger vision. We should never purposefully bury these, especially out of fear or lethargy.

James and John tussle for the prized position of sitting next to Jesus in his 'glory'. These brothers come furtively, without the company of the other disciples – an indication that ambition is often something that feels just a little shameful. They mirror so many conversations, perhaps that we too have had, in which we seek to manipulate ourselves into a prestigious position of favour or power. Interestingly, Jesus does not dismiss their request out of hand but rather unpacks the implications of what they are asking, for ambition walks a costly path of hard work and ironic self-sacrifice.

Ambition becomes problematic when we begin to push others aside to make way for our own glory. It also becomes a spiritual problem when we allow its unfulfillment to sour our souls with bitterness and dissatisfaction. When we do not get the job we were working ourselves up to, or when our best friend gets it instead, it feels easy to let this affect our self-esteem and to rail against life's injustice, or to become cynical at the 'system', whatever this might be.

As God's Son and promised Messiah, Jesus exemplifies inhabiting a vocation without taking on the mantle of ambition. At every stage he refuses to be associated with the mightiness and military power of the anticipated saviour of the Jewish people.

Paul Bradbury describes ambition in this way:

> We are driven to create, to subdue, to use our intellect and ingenuity in the use of the materials we find around us in creation. We often call this ambition. However, we are also created to serve, to surrender, to relate, to offer something of that same self-sacrifice to the wider good, the broader community. Perhaps the word for this is vocation.[4]

Vocation is not a moral alternative to ambition, but it is ambition filtered through a lens of unselfishness, service and self-sacrifice. It also places the glory of God first and foremost, as is demonstrated in Jesus' life, a life lived in paradox, a life that was lost in order to be regained, an element that is not evident in the request of James and John.

In the arts and literature, ambition is a juicy subject. As observers we love to witness a life gone wrong because of a bad power craze. Ambition is one such double-edged theme, and Shakespeare's *Julius Caesar* deals particularly well with its subtleties. As the assassins stand around the slain body of Caesar, Brutus says, 'Ambition's debt is paid.'[5] The assumption is that a man who acts on his ambitions always has a heavy price to pay for doing so. Brutus is drawn into a conspiracy with Cassius, who persuades him that Caesar must be killed because he is about to overthrow the state in order to elevate himself as Roman Emperor. It becomes Brutus' job to explain this to the people, telling them that Caesar's ambitions had to be annihilated for this reason, and yet advocating that this dead and proud man also epitomized many good qualities as well.

One of the most famous speeches in Shakespeare, Marc Antony's 'Friends, Romans, countrymen, lend me your ears', follows, in which Antony denies the presence of bad ambition in Caesar and lists instead his acts of generosity and valour as well as his love for the people of Rome.[6]

Ambition perhaps can be hard to disentangle from good and pure intentions to strive for the best. In *Henry VIII*, Shakespeare implies that it was ambition that made the angels themselves fall from grace into sin.[7]

Like so many grace-filled concepts, ambition can easily turn sour, like milk on a warm day, when the conditions of our lives do not seem so healthy. Edmund Burke says, 'Well is it known that ambition can creep as well as soar.'[8] Yet without ambition, the world would not have achieved the discoveries that space exploration has initiated, we would not have the wealth of knowledge that we have available to us through the internet. Without ambition, apartheid would not have collapsed. Ambition can engender resolute and determined energy and be a force for great goodness as well as great harm. Perhaps, therefore, this is why Jesus states such a categorical 'no' to this final push from his satanical adversary in the wilderness.

Ambition, then, need not be dispensed with, but its aim and focus need to be rinsed through with prayer and discernment on a regular basis as it matures and redeems itself into a new understanding of what vocation means. Reflecting on it another way, perhaps we could say that Jesus is 'vocationally ambitious'. Here is an extraordinary man who feels his divine and driven purpose keenly but who refuses to compromise his own personhood, and instead is prepared to sacrifice his own precious life for the sake of the world's future.

Position

The greatest and the least in God's eyes
(Mark 9.33–37)

The point is to find something that feeds your sense of purpose, and to be willing to look low for that purpose as well as high. It may be chopping wood and it may be running a corporation. Whatever it is, perhaps you will hold open the possibility that doing it is one way to learn what it means to be fully human. (Barbara Brown Taylor)[1]

Keith Lamdin introduces his book, *Finding Your Leadership Style*, with the following story:

A train broke down, causing significant delay. The passengers on the train had no idea when the train would begin to move again and indeed whether they would be able to make their destinations and further connections on time. There aren't many situations in our lives any longer which leave us ultimately powerless, even for a short time, at the mercy of the expertise of others. Speed and the maximum utilization of time are two new gods we worship on a regular basis in our mostly overly busy lives.

On this occasion, the two staff members responsible for the refreshment trolley took it upon themselves to progress up the train to serve everyone a free hot drink. As they did so they chatted to the passengers to provide some human interaction and reassurance from someone official in a uniform.

While these staff members did not have the necessary expertise or authority to get the train moving again, they nevertheless used their own position in extremely effective leadership, utilizing the

67

limitations of their own roles. In those hours when the train was stationary, when people's emotions were degenerating into anger and frustration, the serving of something very simple – tea and kindness – helped to keep morale high and to retain a sense of perspective in the situation. More than anything, as these women concentrated on the pastoral care of each person, they enabled a sense of temporary community to grow, shifting the focus from frustration into something far more positive.[2]

People can be effective leaders in any walk of life, but as Christians we have the responsibility to live good leadership. Leadership upheld and received in this sense can feel like a grace-filled blessing to those both in a faith arena as well as in environments where there is a culture driven by overly rigorous targets and significant financial pressure.

In Mark 9, Jesus encourages his disciples to move away from grappling for power and stigma and instead to move downwards in their understanding of the pecking order. This is another example of the Gospels turning on their heads the values the world often promotes. Followers of Christ look for examples to serve others first and foremost, rather than promoting themselves. The order of the deacon is so important in ordained ministry, with bishops often reminding those newly ordained never to forget Christ's charge to be servants. Children, so often ignored, relegated and swept aside (certainly in Jesus' day), are to be understood as being the key to this overturning of the world and its values.

In our own spheres and communities there are opportunities that we ourselves can decisively take which can be positive and humble approaches to our positions, whatever they might be. Maybe we find ourselves being parents of difficult, unmotivated children, or leading churches that believe their golden age lies firmly in the past and are stuck in the rut of a 'can't change' mentality. Perhaps our work team is bored and has been tasked to come up with an impossibly dynamic strategy to salvage the firm's future, or we are part of the teaching staff of a seriously underperforming school.

How can a 'position' be used to become a grace-filled blessing for those who might be finding their own positions untenable? Encouragement can reap enormous rewards. Words of genuine affirmation can provide renewed sustenance, like a good nutrient to a hothouse flower, enabling it to unfurl to its maximum beauty and potential. When the going gets tough, introducing perspective, so that people retain a sense of their whole lives, the belief and hope that there is space and potential to do a great many things, can also water someone's wilderness, perhaps particularly at work.

It is also about using whatever power we have in our position to support those who are the least as well as the lost. Sharing personal experience – of the successes we have enjoyed as well as the failures and uncertainties – often provides an enormous sense of hope for others.

These are all ways that Jesus uses his position as a leader effectively and bravely, as prophet, Messiah, charismatic and mystical Son of God. Christ gathers others who walk in his wake and who are drawn to his inspiring leadership because he lives within this in such a distinctively different way from how this concept is understood within the leadership of the day.

Jesus is our archetypal ideal regarding leadership in the sense of how to inhabit a position well. Part of the groundedness of this is that his own leadership is earthed, sometimes appearing stern and authoritarian. But inspired by a power far greater than himself, he draws constantly on the dynamism as well as the comfort of *ruach*, God's Holy Spirit. He lives out of humility as he washes the dusty and gnarled feet of his friends, but he is also unafraid to stand up to the bullying authority of those who are secretly threatened by his message and holiness. He gathers followers but refuses to be put on a pedestal and worshipped. His leadership comes in the form of encouragement as well as from a place of challenge, regardless of personal consequences. He refuses to be defensive or to make others the scapegoat, but takes upon himself all that is unjust and corrupt amid a tyrannical state system and dishonourable religious elite.

Thomas Merton offers some wisdom on this subject:

Do not depend on the hope of results. You may have to face the fact that your work will be apparently worthless and even achieve no result at all, if not perhaps results the opposite to what you expect. As you get used to this idea, you start more and more to concentrate not on the results, but on the value, the rightness, the truth of the work itself. You gradually struggle less and less for an idea and more and more for specific people. In the end, it is the reality of *personal relationship* that saves everything.[3]

Good leadership, therefore, always has at its heart the consideration and care of others. If promotion happens and ambition is satisfied despite this, then there is nothing wrong with the fulfilment of our God-given potential, but it must never happen at the expense, or deliberately to the detriment, of others.

Contribution

The widow's mite
(Luke 21.1–4)

Some frustration over a glitch with online shopping recently led me to do some serious reflection on people working in call centres. I reflected too on those who contribute to our society and lifestyle a great deal but who often remain in the background and sometimes unpopular: those who collect our copious amounts of refuse, warehouse staff and traffic wardens, to name but a few.

In the instance of my online shopping frustration, when someone is just a voice on the end of the phone, it becomes easier for me to vent my frustration. It's easy to forget that a person's employment security is bound up in how helpful and courteous they are to me as a consumer, however rude I may be.

Yet people in call centres who sort out our minute as well as our monumental frustrations contribute significantly to what often feels like an overly complex society. Trying to obtain a refund for a misplaced item, I resorted to a 'live chat'. Within 30 minutes my problem had been resolved, my anger abated and an irritation was ticked off my 'to do' list; my day felt a few degrees better.

Jesus' interaction with the world and its people is all about the small things of life, often the small things that make a difference. The tiny pearl that is hugely valuable, the one leper who says 'thank you' out of a group of ten, the sparrow that falls to the ground noticed and loved by God even though there are millions the world over. The passage in the Synoptic Gospels known as the widow's mite has become enshrined in popular history as a metaphor for the power of such a small contribution when it stems from utter poverty as well as loving faithfulness. After several parables about the proper approach and use of money, Jesus uses this short snapshot to contrast with the preceding verses, which are a diatribe against the hypocrisy of the teachers of the law and their apparent piety and status. He contrasts the honest transparency of the widow with their nonsense and desire to be visually noticed, the sham of being holy as well as the reality of their unconcern for the poor.

The *mite* or *lepta* was an actual form of currency. Two of these equalled a *quadran*, the smallest of the Roman coins. Jesus uses this incident to highlight the power and significance of the woman's gift put into the temple coffers, and to contrast it with the casual and meaningless giving of the rich and powerful, who donate from a place of comfort and plenty. So often in the Gospels Jesus tells stories about supposedly tiny contributions and interactions that have immense significance. A very small amount of faith, of belief in who *he* is, for example, is sufficient to unlock the life of someone who is sick, blind, paralysed or beaten down. Being a grace-filled person is all about how the heart is positioned, how a situation is approached and understood.

Most of us can recall times involving real-life widows and their contributions. The person on the edge of our church who finally agrees to come to the Harvest Supper and who brings something beautifully cooked to contribute to the feast. I had a good friend who was a single mum of three. She never had very much money, but her children were friends with mine and they would always be invited to my son's birthday parties. The presents my son received from his friend (her son) had much less monetary value than the crisp £10 notes, vouchers and toys he would receive from wealthier parents, and while we were grateful for all of these, her small bag of chocolates were the presents I most remember and gratefully appreciated.

Seemingly small things can feel immense, beautiful and special – things and experiences to be treasured, noticed and remembered. This is what Jesus suggests as he witnesses this event – that the larger coins of the religious leaders and the wealthy land at the bottom of the temple coffers with a hollow thud, while the widow's small 'mites', with their bright jingle, are heard far more loudly in heaven.

Fans of the recent BBC One series *Poldark* will have been mesmerized as well as frustrated by the long-standing love between privileged Morwenna and poor yokel-boy Drake Carne. In a previous season, Drake gives to Morwenna, out of his poverty, a small handmade bracelet which has no financial value whatsoever. But because it has been given to her by him, with such expansive love, she treasures it throughout her unhappy and abusive marriage to the Revd Osborne Whitworth.

It's interesting to note that Jesus does not rush up to the widow and tell her not to contribute or that it is not necessary. Despite her poverty this woman believes she has something to give, even if she has been wrongfully manipulated into giving it. Jesus has no desire to take away the choice and power of individual decision, and neither does God, for all such contributions are valued by him when they are made with love. Ironically, the widow gives a contribution out of her poverty into another's wealth, which is not really wealth at all but greed and ostentation. Yet because she gives regardless of this, she retains her dignity and the little power she still has, and perhaps this is the reason why Jesus doesn't try to stop her doing what she does.

Most of us, when we give, give half-heartedly. We do this for a variety of understandable reasons: we feel anxious about money and we have other demands on our resources. We are not told how the widow feels as she drops her money into the temple coffers – relief at doing the expected and correct thing, a genuine sense of contribution, or maybe resentment? But what we can be assured of is that whatever her own attitude is, this is giving from a wilderness place: as a widow she is without a husband and therefore on the bottom rung of the social ladder. Her so-called offering is a sacrifice because, as Jesus intimates, she would have few resources of her own.

Mother Teresa offers us that brilliant glimpse of accessibility in terms of the contributions we make: 'We can do not great things, only small things with great love. It is not how much you do but how much love you put into doing it.'[1]

This is a basis for reflection on the contribution we make in our lives, and on whether there are ever any occasions when we give sacrificially out of our own poverty, however we classify this, completely and utterly as the widow did. Yet in right discernment and attitude we inadvertently step into grace, because to truly give feels so rightly loving. Jesus himself gives in this way and is the sign to us that when we contribute sacrificially, when we are entirely 'spent', then miracles happen, and lives can be transformed.

Vocation

Jesus appears to Mary Magdalene (John 20.1–18)

Our vocation is to live in the Spirit – not to be more and more remarkable animals.
(Metropolitan Anthony Bloom, 1914–2003)[1]

A colleague, Ann, a permanent deacon and former psychiatric nurse, tells the true and extraordinary story of Mary, whom she regularly cared for in one of the UK's former mental asylums. Mary had entered this institution in her teens and was now in her nineties, so she had spent almost her entire life in the hospital. She had been silent for the whole of this time until, one night, as Ann was preparing her for bed, Mary spoke. In an extraordinary moment, Mary foretold that her death would take place that night and she asked Ann to pray with her. Mary did indeed die that night, after also uttering the most incredible words: 'Tonight I know that I am going to fulfil my own calling with God, that which I have not yet been able to do.'

The reason why Mary had been incarcerated at such a young age was that she had expressed the call to become a priest. At the time, this was considered an utterly preposterous, even scandalous, suggestion for a young woman, and Mary was subsequently shut away. She had vowed to be silent until such a time that her vocation could be complete. Mary's frustrated vocation somehow mysteriously echoed that which was also beginning to emerge within Ann herself.[2]

Vocation is powerful. The word comes from the Latin *vocare*, meaning 'to call'. It suggests an external power (which Christians understand as God 'calling' through the Holy Spirit) which invites something inside us to a life of deep-seated loving service and fulfilment. There are myriad different experiences of 'calling', from the dramatic Damascus Road blinding light to the quieter still, small voice. People describe dreams and visions, a nagging push or pull of simply wanting to do more for God, as well as a desire to be alongside others at pivotal moments, a yearning to participate in a sacramental ministry but mostly just trying to be a 'means of grace' for others. Individuals often feel unworthy as well as strangely intrepid, astonished that God is asking them to do something new and often frightening, as so many of the biblical characters did. Vocation is often an unknown journey which involves humility as well as courage.

Vocation ebbs and flows, grows and changes, just as other things in life do. Often within one personhood we hold a variety of things we feel deeply and passionately called to do. We might feel we have a vocation to be a foster parent as well as our day job as a chef, preparing and delighting people with good food. We might not have the luxury of 'vocation' in our work, but our hinterland time becomes the place where we find the most meaning.

A friend of mine is an extraordinarily talented artist. In order to paint he has converted the attic of his ex-council house into the archetypical artist's studio. His day job is working at a centre for the homeless, and while this is rewarding as well as demanding, it is not his ultimate vocation; painting is. He once described to me how this felt, that his artistic expression was something like a compulsion, almost an addiction, an occupation he felt he simply had to do however tired or uninspired he was. Vocation is being mysteriously drawn to do things for the sake of the divine, mesmerized to implement some kind of expression of love.

Vocation is not always something that emanates from ourselves. Biblical vocation is often suggested, even commanded, by God, catalysing and recalibrating someone to change their way of life to become absorbed in God's plans. Jesus invites many on to a new journey, often without any prior sense of vocation.

In John 20, Mary Magdalene is drawn, compelled, to go to look for Jesus, even though rationally she knows he is dead. Vocation often feels highly improbable, even crazy, but people do something anyway, often putting their whole lives in trust to God.

When Mary does encounter the risen Christ walking in the garden, he calls her by her name. Many stories of vocation begin with God calling people by their names, vocation being a highly individual experience with no two stories being the same.

Mary Magdalene is charged to become effectively the first evangelist, as she goes to tell the rest of the disciple band that Jesus is risen and alive in the world and potentially in every heart. Mark and Luke both record resurrection appearances where Magdalene and other women with her are not initially believed (Mark 16.11; Luke 24.11). Vocation can be costly. It is not so simple as to presume that just because we are 'called' by God to do something, an easy and smooth pathway lies ahead, as the story of Mary so clearly demonstrates.

Lent and Holy Week describe the ultimate vocation which belongs to Jesus as God's only Son, his time in the wilderness girding him with spiritual iron to walk the costly and terrifying journey to death and ultimate resurrection. Often people are called to undertake hard and difficult tasks and roles but feel compelled nevertheless to do them. But vocation is also never about personal achievement, and in this way it is distinctively different from ambition. We might feel drawn to climb Mount Everest and, although impressive, even potentially record breaking, this remains a personal achievement rather than anything to do with vocation. Vocation is always associated with using our gifts and skills for the service of others for the glory of God.

Vocation is also about the attitude and approach we take to the things we are occupied with in our lives. It is usually the realization that a job is far more than 'just a job'; that it has become something more demanding, tiring and costly; something that takes us far beyond being a 'jobsworth'. A vocational approach often means that others notice what we do and how we inhabit our 'role', and that it also brings us a deep sense of joy. It is a siren call that we cannot ignore, and we are drawn by its deep magic which means we just want to keep immersing ourselves in it.

Vocation emerges from a sincere belief that God is asking something of us at a particular time. In many lives, however, vocation may be unrecognized, but we nevertheless still feel an innate sense of satisfaction within an existing way of life or occupation where love is the driving force.

Part of the wilderness the younger generation experience these days is the underlying anxiety of whether they will find a secure job in life or not. The trajectory for those who are bright and gifted while at school is often one that feels overly pressurized. So often choices are made on the strength of how much money someone will earn rather than an occupation or a role someone passionately wants to do. Vocation needs to be reinstated in the life of our education system far more than it currently is, with cogent discussions about how an individual life can contribute to a wider community and world. If we are privileged to have the choice about how we live our lives (for so many in our world do not), then it seems that we also have a responsibility to ask and to keep asking ourselves what our vocation at the present moment is or could be as we move through our lives.

Service

Jesus washes the disciples' feet (John 13.1–17)

If the glory of God is to break out in your service, you must be
ready to go out into the night.
(Basilea Schlink, 1904–2001)[1]

The idea of service is one that potentially every Christian is
challenged to take up, and it connects all the concepts within this
chapter. When we become members of the body of Christ at our
baptism, and if we are serious about following Jesus, we are signing
up for a life of service. Jesus tells his followers to love God and love
our neighbour (Mark 12.29–31), but how we do this is worked out in
myriad creative and prosaic ways across the globe.

Service can be embedded in ambition, it forms a part of contribution as well as position and is an inevitable part of vocation.
Service is a sign of hope to a crumbling and disillusioned world, it
restores faith in humanity and often also in God and it operates as a
catch-all dynamic when other institutions are at breaking-point in
terms of what they can offer a careworn society.

The archetypal passage about service during the season of Lent is
Jesus washing the feet of his disciples in John 13. In ancient Palestine,
this action would have been reserved for the lowliest of all servants.
Feet would not have been pedicured and washed regularly as they are
in our own time, but dusty and fetid. More than anything, it would
require servants to stoop low, to physically be on a different level
from those whose feet they washed. The symbol proves to be such
a powerful metaphor still and is now translated into Street Pastors

distributing flip-flops to inebriated clubbers on weekend nights in town centres, clergy shining shoes or undertaking an equivalent lowly act of service publicly, often on Maundy Thursday itself.

Service spans disciplines, practices and faiths, potentially uniting those who have a faith with those who might not claim any belief at all. At the heart of service must be a deep love for others, for service ceases to become powerful if we do it for the wrong reasons.

The recent film *The Children Act* (2017) models a variety of different ways of serving. Fiona Maye is a High Court Judge who is involved in several high-profile cases involving children. She works hard, going over and above her duty to try to see justice prevail in a number of cases. But Fiona's marriage is in crisis and she uses overwork to shut away the emotions that inevitably arise from such a situation. Also in the film is her loyal clerk, Nigel, who meticulously cares for her every professional need without any verbal gratitude or recognition. There is a beautiful moment when one of the nurses wipes the tears away from the cheek of Adam Henry, a Jehovah's Witness teenager whom Fiona has gone to visit in hospital to come to a decision about whether the court should rule an enforced blood transfusion. It is a tender snapshot of the service as well as the vocation of nursing.

In John 13, Jesus is not asked to wash feet. This is certainly not something that would be expected of someone who has grown respect as a strong leader and mystic among disciples and others. The preceding passage (John 12.49–50) speaks of an understood and embedded power that Jesus is aware of within himself. It is this power, purified into a confidence, that undertakes the countercultural act that he undertakes. It is unprecedented as well as unprovoked: Jesus simply gets up and begins to wash the feet of those he is closest to. His actions surprise, shock and eventually challenge, the loudest objection coming from Peter.

Jesus does this to model a way of behaving which he wants the disciples, as the inheritors of his ministry, to take seriously. It is of paramount importance that they understand the significance of what he has done for them, as he insistently asks in verses 12–17. Although Jesus takes the traditional line about slaves not being greater than their masters, he completely subverts this through his own actions, making a powerful statement about the equality and dignity of those who live within God's realm. Indeed, this gesture moves beyond a gesture of humility and reveals the nature of God himself.

Ghislaine Howard's intimate image of Jesus washing Peter's feet portrays two figures, dressed in simple Middle Eastern attire, who dominate the composition. This could be the moment Peter remonstrates with his master, or the painting could be read as this act of service somehow unlocking a conversation and spiritual awakening which happens anyway in Peter's shifting perspective. Howard mixed sand with paint to give the surface of the work a sculptural texture, a physical symbol of the earthed and intimate physicality of such an act of hospitality.[2]

When the newly ordained become deacons in the Church of England, there is an emphasis on being a servant to the Church and the world and specifically serving the community in which they are set. A particularly poignant phrase in the Ordination Rite reads, 'reaching into the forgotten corners of the world, that the love of God may be made visible'. A question to ask is, 'Where are the forgotten corners in your own life, in your own context, which need some love to be injected into them?'

Jesus challenges us to be continuously awake to those who live in such forgotten corners, to that of which much of the world remains purposefully ignorant or disregarding. Forgotten corners are not just the lonely behind closed doors, but those we really would rather not wish to consider because they are held to be unacceptable and unpleasant. Jean Vanier, with his profound insight into working with people with learning disabilities, says:

Peter has an understanding of society as a pyramid: at the top there is power, riches, privileges, and hopefully wisdom. At the bottom are slaves, people who have no function, people with disabilities, and immigrants. However, Jesus has another vision of the community that he will build: he will build a *body*. In this body, each person has a place – even the weakest parts. Even the most vulnerable and fragile members are important, and each one is called to become a friend of Jesus.[3]

So much of service is about practical acts, and these are something we are all capable of and involved with, for we are all physical
beings, needing to do stuff for others and to have things done for
us too. A close friend of mine takes in teenagers in crisis under the
umbrella of an agency that deals with emergency overnight provision. This is risky and costly, but it is not only a ministry she can
offer which is offset by the stability of her own family, it is also a
service that emphasizes the interconnectedness we have with one
another; it has the potential to link that which we assume divides
us – class, age, race, sexuality. Through simple, practical acts of
service, relationship is built and becomes perfumed and holy, as
it did when the unknown woman poured perfume all over Jesus.
Through service activated by love, God is always experienced, even
if he is not always named or recognized.

Prayer and action

- What are the occupations you hold within your life? How do these relate to the use of your time? Reflect on or discuss the poem at the beginning of the chapter. Do you identify with any of the images within it? Pray for the right use of your time. Pray for those who have time to do what they really want to do as well as for those who struggle to find direction and meaning in their lives. How could the church community help?
- Do you consider yourself ambitious? Where has this led and left you so far in your life? How have you experienced the impact of other people's ambitions in your own life and work? Do you have an example of 'right ambition' and what this looks like? Pray for those whose dreams and yearnings remain unfulfilled.
- Reflect on those whose position in their private or public lives remains insecure. Pray for those whose families are affected by this.
- Which leaders have you most admired in your life? Can you find examples of good leadership in seemingly lowly positions, reflecting on the story at the beginning of this chapter?
- How do you contribute to God's kingdom – at home, in your place of work, in your community, in church? Is there a prompting to do more or something different? Can you find examples of even the smallest contribution like the widow's mite being cogent and significant, and are there right ways of highlighting this to inspire others in our churches?
- Are you aware of having your own 'vocation'? Is this difficult to identify or talk about? If so, is there someone who can help you

develop this? Are you aware of anyone around you having a gift or yearning to do something? Could *you* be a part of their flourishing?

- How do you serve God? Where do you see people 'washing feet' around you?

WEEK 4

Introduction: freedom

The truth that brings ultimate freedom (John 8.31–38)

Walking in freedom

Over many miles of wild terrain,
He collects the stones and dust of the road
On the soles of his shoes.
And he carries
The burden of love in his heart.
As birds sing their daily freshness
He remembers a time when he was carefree,
Unexhausted by life's load and muck.
But on this delicious morning
He breathes the balmy oxygen
And walks
Out onto the hills
As worries fall away,
Like a silk gown from body, and
Freedom comes.[1]

I've got a relatively new job and I love my commute to work. After arriving at Waterloo Station, I walk past the London Eye and across Westminster Bridge. The water of the Thames is alive with activity, and on this bright morning the bridge pulsates with life, a vibrant smorgasbord of human activity. There are groups of tourists delighted to be in the capital, taking selfies with the Houses of Parliament glinting in the sunshine behind them. Groups of schoolchildren are enjoying exciting trips to see the sights. *The Big*

Issue sellers and buskers – everyone from magicians to bagpipe players – and rickshaw drivers loiter; policemen and women and ordinary people like me are trying to get to work.

As I walk, I feel the warmth of the thin air which heralds the spring after months of cold and wet. I am free, my heart soars and I feel genuinely lucky to be alive, grateful for so many good things in my life. But as I cross Parliament Square, I walk past numerous (Brexit) demonstrations, and am reminded that my life is not completely independent or worry free because it is bound up with so much that is connected with the opinions and decisions of others – always. Forces and passions outside my control do and always will have a bearing upon how I live my life as well as the quality of it.

Living in freedom is different within every culture, society and religion; it is distinctive, too, in every age and context. As contemporary people living in the western hemisphere, we may feel as though we can never completely relax, that we are always in some ways constrained. CCTV is everywhere: our words and actions are noticed and monitored at work and in the public eye. In the so-called developed world, we enjoy the apparent privileges of untold freedoms far more than in other centuries, and we also ponder what the implications of these might be for us and whether these lead us ultimately into wilderness rather than grace. The freedom to not hold any religious views means that many people swim in a vacuum of not knowing where to turn when crisis hits. In a plethora of individual choices, where do we find our moral compass, no longer backlit by the reference point of faith? Ubiquitous choice in so many areas of our lives can leave us feeling overwhelmed and exhausted, yet we often rail against the removal of such choices, for whatever reason.

A life lived in Christ is one that does not deny the inevitable constraints of human living, but one that instead puts these in second place as it follows a distinctively deeper narrative, as John 8 describes. To be free is not as simple as walking out of prison once and for all. We are forever creating false gods and listening to alluring voices that seek to constrain us. We are influenced by other people and the irrational fear of what might happen to us and, as we travel through life, we collect the 'stuff of the road', as the above poem, 'Walking in freedom', explains. It describes the experience that one man has of sensing the exhilaration of momentary freedom through the act of walking one spring day when the atmosphere is hazy, and the air refreshes his soul, which is tired from the feelings of hurts and responsibilities that weigh him down.

This chapter reflects on themes that connect with the concept of **freedom**. Jesus is someone who crosses many a **boundary** – physically, emotionally and spiritually – in order to release people from the prisons that hold them back from flourishing. Today we are a country obsessed with boundary, the idea that there is a line that guards and protects a sense of 'home' and all the privileges that go with it. With this comes a preoccupation with our personal and communal **safety** – an experience that halts our freedom to move towards others in friendship rather than suspicion. Newer anxieties also lurk, such as the fear of whether we will be the next unfortunate victim of a bombing on the Underground as we cross the capital – or indeed anywhere. The question is, do we allow ourselves to be incapacitated and to become paranoid, or do we approach our lives in a spirit of adventure and as a gift in trust, with the knowledge that, whatever happens to us, all is ultimately bound up in God's embrace?

In the Passion Narrative, the **denial** of Peter and the crowd resonates with our own denial to embrace both the cost and the freedom of a life lived in Christ. We deny because it seems easier, or because we are frightened or embarrassed of the implications that faith and love might bring, just as Peter was. But in the end our protestations only seek to suppress our yearning to follow Jesus, in the deep knowledge that the gospel brings a strange freedom into our tired lives.

Moving away from this and towards grace comes **repentance**, when we genuinely turn ourselves around to shed the things from the past and the present which bind us to the totem of false values and the lies we so easily tell and believe, to ourselves and others.

As a Jew, Jesus could live his life as an obscure carpenter, but a life of radical service which challenges the existing norms of the day is the one he walks. The Gospels present an extraordinary life, one which through the power of the Holy Spirit is spent freeing others from the constraints they find themselves locked within. Jesus heals people from physical illnesses, disabilities and disfigurements. Introducing a new perspective on the world, he affirms the new freedom people can discover through God's kingdom, particularly those whose social status is zero: the women who anoint him with oil, the Samaritan woman at the well and the beggars who sit at the entrance to the city. Yet freedom does not come at any cost – it is bound up with the need for repentance and emerging and fragile faith, but is always based on grace rather than righteousness. Often Jesus offers a **choice**, as choice is part of this decisive step into freedom. The young man of great wealth withdraws after his encounter with Christ, as he knows, sadly, that he does not possess the strength of character to leave all his wealth behind to follow Jesus unencumbered.

There is mystery as well as paradox in freedom. Sacrificing our own freedom and choices often releases a greater degree in the lives of others, as the story of the good Samaritan and the prodigal son demonstrate. God loves the world in freedom, yet such freedom gave rise to tragedy in the world – that first manipulative and decisive act of defiance in the plucking of the apple from the tree in the Garden of Eden.

The South African priest Ananias Mpunzi says that freedom is never static but always a process, and this reflects the mysterious freedom with which God approaches the world: 'Our task is to look for the structures that can support freedom, though the structures themselves are not freedom. But they will be structures which are flexible and adaptable as the human beings they are designed to serve.'[2]

Our own freedom and the choices we have should be held carefully as sacred privileges, to be approached and filtered through the heart and spirit of Christ and the way he inhabits the freedom he is both given and denied.

Boundary

The raising of Lazarus
(John 11.1–44)

In preparing the ground for mending relationships, Jesus quite
often defies established boundaries and invites his followers to
demonstrate radical openness. He brings people of different
cultures and orientations closer to one another – his way of
disciple-making being a great example.
(Muthuraj Swamy)[1]

The border . . . G80: that vast non-existent territory where
freedom and metamorphosis are common currency.
(Roberto Bolaño (adapted))[2]

As I left home for the first time, the parameters of childhood suddenly did not feel so strong. All that had previously boundaried my
life now no longer carried the weight that it had before. Student life
presented the possibilities of new adventures in relationships, as a
cohort of friendship became marvellously available from a much
wider demographic. The boundaries of the student house were also
fluid as we regularly slept on one another's sofas and floors after late
nights of drinking and conversation.

Politically, the late 1980s was a time when some powerful symbols
of oppressive boundaries were disintegrating around the world.
My boyfriend of the time sped off to Germany in 1989 as the Berlin
Wall came down, yearning to witness this momentous event,
himself crossing several national borders to do so and even bringing
his individual piece of the Wall back home! Dispensing with that

particularly powerful boundary brought liberation to many who had for years been barred from entering a part of their own country. These were the years, too, that Nelson Mandela and others who strived for the dismantling of the apartheid regime were released after lengthy periods of incarceration, and as students we marched in celebratory triumph as the infrastructure of the laws that had oppressed South Africa began to seriously disintegrate.

Such an implicit sense of solidarity is particularly important today, and Muthuraj Swamy identifies why it is so vital, associating the crossing of boundaries with potential reconciliation, or a lack of it:

> This approach is important because we have to deal today not only with broken relationships between those who once were friends but also with the systemic brokenness of relationships among wider communities. We live in an environment where people are not prepared to relate to those who are different.[3]

Boundaries are physical, emotional and spiritual. They can also be political, just as they were in Jesus' day. Boundaries mark territory, protect and prevent. They enable people to understand what is allowable and acceptable, even if this may be hotly contested. Upbringing, professional training, and cultural and religious identities all establish codes of conduct and often unspoken behavioural boundaries. Boundaries do not always protect, but they do help us understand where the intention behind them resides and who instigates this – to not trespass, to not assume the right to live somewhere, to not take advantage. Potentially, boundaries are liberating as well as oppressive. And even after years of establishment they can disintegrate to nothing, remaining a shadow of history.

In the world today, there are still notorious and contentious boundaries. The 'Mexican Wall' is one that runs over vast distances in the United States of America. This south-west border wall has been erected as part of the current US zero-tolerance policy on illegal immigration, which has left more than 2,000 immigrant children separated from their families, creating international outrage and protest. Congressman Vicente Gonzalez is a controversial voice against the completion of this wall, arguing that it is a regressional step in terms of the values and history of the American people. It is stated that the wall is a wasteful use of billions of dollars of taxpayers' money, is profoundly unkind to those seeking residency and asylum and is potentially detrimental to the natural environment wherever it is constructed.[4]

The Lenten journey ends with the greatest boundary issue of all time – the death and resurrection of Jesus – as God breaks through the barriers that human fear holds us within to release everlasting and extraordinary new life. During his own lifetime Jesus breaks down barriers and pushes religious, political and spiritual boundaries. He destabilizes existing boundaries when he believes these to be keeping a person imprisoned, usually through the value system that has been foisted upon them or through an impoverished sense of self-worth. He heals those considered unclean according to Jewish purity laws, he allows dubious women to pour perfume over him and touch his body, and he physically moves from place to place, as a Jew himself, into the badlands of the Gentiles.

The raising of Lazarus in John 11 marks the final miracle Jesus undertakes before his journey to the cross. The story anticipates Jesus' own pathway, with love being the connecting factor. As one of only three people whom Jesus raises from the dead, Lazarus is someone Jesus *loves*.

God loves the world and invites humanity to live a different life through the possibilities that the resurrection of Christ brings. The Jews believe in the resurrection of the dead on the last day, as Martha mentions in verse 24. The resurrection happens through Christ himself: in his very personhood he removes a boundary, symbolized in the ripping of the temple curtain. Anyone who lives in submission to Christ has already passed from death to life (John 5.24).

Interestingly, this miracle happens in a place where Jesus is *protected* by a physical boundary: verse 8 tells readers that the Jews want to kill Jesus, presumably because they have had enough of his challenging of established boundaries through his powerful but subversive ministry. The raising of Lazarus happens away from the province of Jerusalem, which makes it legally difficult for the Jews to arrest Jesus.

While the crowd shouted about a smelly and unhygienic body he, perhaps sensibly, hesitates to enter the tomb, choosing not to cross this particular boundary. Through the dialogue between the sisters and Jesus, the boundary of faith is also lived through, as Jesus tells Martha that she must believe in him if she is to understand the glory of God. Jesus' handling of and interaction with emotional, spiritual and religious boundaries in this passage bring new life for one human being. Lent challenges us to reflect on the concept of boundary and where boundaries might be situated within our own lives.

Boundaries create freedom because they enable us to feel secure. But they also stimulate a sense of injustice and frustration at an often questionable wielding of power in terms of who creates and establishes them, as the demonstrations across the globe against the American immigration policy reveal.

A faith-based approach to boundary should be to ask: What is its purpose, and is this based on a compassionate outcome? Whose freedom is the boundary protecting? Do boundaries or the dismantling of them positively transform lives or not?

Boundaries are needed for our own self-care and well-being, and our personal and national safety. But they are usually ambiguous and often feel archaic, inappropriate and oppressive, an anti-kingdom phenomenon which builds on an 'us and them' mentality of alien 'otherness'. The German biblical scholar Walter Brueggemann says this:

> The Jordan looms as a decisive boundary in the Bible, laden with symbolic power. It is the boundary between the precariousness of the wilderness and the confidence of at-home-ness. The crossing of the Jordan is the most momentous experience that could happen to Israel, representing the moment of the most radical transformation of any historical person or group, the moment of empowerment or enlandment, the decisive event of being turfed and at home for the first time.[5]

A journey through boundary potentially becomes an experience of grace.

Safety

Those who love their life lose it, and those who hate their life in this world will keep it for eternal life (John 12.25–26)

The dangers of life are infinite, and among them is safety.
(Johann Wolfgang von Goethe, 1749–1832)[1]

On the surface, Jesus' statement in John 12 might suggest a joyless approach to the gift of life. But he is talking about priority. The lives of his followers are not to be constrained by safety, security or comfort. If we are prepared to give up some of these 'rights' (although they are normal and understandable), then we see very perceptively into the nature of God's alternative reality of the kingdom.

That said, most human beings need their reference points, where safety begins with a sense of belonging. A place to call 'home' – a place where we feel socially, politically and culturally surrounded by people who 'feel like us' is a deep-seated subconscious need. In her recent autobiography, Michelle Obama describes the often painful and tiring experience of being among the black minority at an Ivy League University: 'It's hard to put into words what you sometimes pick up in the ether, the quiet, cruel nuances of not belonging – the subtle cues that tell you to not risk anything, to find your people and just stay put.'[2]

Feeling safe goes far beyond not needing to always watch our backs at the cashpoint; it means we and those we care for are secure and content enough to truly flourish wherever we find ourselves. But does our age of anxiety mean that we subconsciously absorb all kinds of messages and information which destabilize those things which previously have been taken as givens? Do we now feel more insecure and unsafe generally in twenty-first-century Britain, and worry that however we understand its noble stability and identity, this is beginning to fall? The random and varied nature of terrorism might give people the excuse never to step outside their front door. In the aftermath of two horrific attacks on students in the USA, our airwaves are full of the vocabulary of gun and hate crime and societies that will soon be inundated with migrants from faraway lands. Ironically, though, we are safer than we ever were before, as our lives are recorded on CCTV, the government protects major public events which are now understood as potential for terrorist attacks, there is no room for sexual crimes to be swept under the carpet, and strong physical as well as legal barriers are built around our pragmatic as well as irrational fears.

It is exhausting to live life without some degree of safety and security. Even Jesus enjoys a place of reference: he has a nationality, home, parents, a following. Strategically he avoids certain areas (Judea and Jerusalem) until the last months of his life, when a holy and obedient zeal drives him on to confront the weakness and evil of the existing religious authorities and the Roman state. From Palm Sunday onwards, his life becomes increasingly unsafe. Followers of Jesus relive that journey, often daily, if they have chosen to put their own right to safety aside in order to speak out or protest against injustice that destabilizes the status quo.

Fear develops through a misunderstanding as well as an idealization of a past where somehow national identity and 'home' are equated with ethnic purity. This in itself can become an unhealthy preoccupation, a harking back to a utopia that never existed. Mohsin Hamid's novel, *Exit West*, explores some of these tensions. Set in an unknown country, it is the love story of two people, Saeed and Nadia, who meet in an evening class in an unnamed city. Having experienced joy within his own family, Saeed is more rooted to his community, while Nadia is running away from an oppressive and war-torn childhood. Together they become wayfaring nomads, journeying to different cities around the world.

In a radio interview, Hamid describes the book as one that explores the concept of arrival rather than the experience of the treacherous journeys that refugees often make. He believes that migrants bravely make and remake their stories many times, which becomes a dynamic that all of us, in our own ways, also live out: 'everyone is a refugee from their childhoods. We step out of our front door everyday into a foreign country.'³ By this he means that our society is changing its make-up continuously, and perhaps always has. There was never a utopian golden age of pure race, English gentility, community stability and comprehensive comfortableness.

Living an authentically Christian life can also never be or feel entirely 'safe', for God invites us to live out of a place of courage and risk for the sake of loving and serving others, however that might be worked out. We are challenged to live in trust, to resist having to be fully in control of our futures. At a time when barriers are bigger than bridges, people of faith can live counterculturally, perhaps choosing to decisively embrace and absorb others' anxieties of unsafety and to question them.

Crossing Birmingham's Invisible Borders (2018) was an inspiring BBC documentary about Aysha Iqbal, a young Muslim woman who decided to step out of the safety of her own, often self-contained, neighbourhood of Balsall Heath, Birmingham, to create a friendship group with women from a very different community. Druid's Heath is just four miles down the road, with a more established white working-class demographic and holding something of an unfair reputation.⁴

Iqbal is involved in helping Muslim women to learn English and empowering them to integrate effectively into the British environment. She happened to be in London on the day of the Westminster Bridge attack in March 2017, which left six dead and 49 injured. This, coupled with the fact that her own brother bears the emotional scars of a racist attack, made her even more determined to promote integration and peace within a mounting culture of fear and prejudice. The documentary demonstrated her visionary courage to establish friendship rather than live in fear and ignorance.

As he journeys to the cross, Jesus' message to the world is that being a child of the kingdom does not guarantee a safe or an easy life. We walk into unknown territory every day, but we choose whether to be incapacitated by a fearful prejudice or to decisively embrace difference and a changing world, believing that we will be stretched, and greater people for our encounter with it, and maybe even discover a way of belonging in fresh ways. The challenge comes when we presuppose that our own right to belonging, rootedness and safety somehow outweighs other people's rights to these things too.

Denial

Jesus before Caiaphas the High Priest, and where Peter denies associations with Jesus (John 18)

Everything was perfectly healthy and normal here in Denial Land.
(Jim Butcher, *Cold Days*)[1]

The former Franciscan priest and recovering alcoholic Brennan Manning (1934–2013) tells the story of the brutal unravelling of a fellow patient at a rehabilitation centre in Minneapolis when he himself was a member of the same group.

One of the hardest, but most crucial, first steps in addiction recovery is the admission by the person that he or she has a problem with dependence. Manning narrates the occasion when Max, a member of his group, stubbornly refused to be transparent about his addiction and was eventually brought low by his therapist coordinator. A call to Max's wife, put on speakerphone for the whole room to hear, described the tragic occasion when Max stopped off at a tavern one winter's night to get a drink. Leaving his nine-year-old daughter Debbie in a locked and rapidly freezing car, Max bumped into some old army friends. Overcome with joy at seeing them again, he lost track of time as well as the responsibility he had to his daughter. When he stumbled back to his car hours later, Debbie was so cold that her ears and some of her fingers had become badly frostbitten, resulting in her being deaf for the rest of her life.

After this story was told and after much adamant denial, Max broke down in front of the group. A hard tactic (hopefully not used in this way today) but one based on tough love and a mirror held up, as Max stepped into courage and eventually acknowledged the reality that he was a man in desperate need of help.

However we might understand the power of evil or the capacity human beings have to pretend to themselves, Manning describes it as a power that 'varnishes the truth and encourages dishonesty'.[2] In 1 John 1.8, all Christians are reminded that we should be wary of denying that we are sinners, for if we do then we are not people of the truth.

Most of us live daily with dishonesty. We tell little white lies for a smoother life, and often to manage complex pressures and responsibilities. But more than this, we live life with different levels of honesty, often pretending to ourselves that things are not as bad as they seem as well as having the continual capacity to deny the more prickly and challenging parts of our own and others' natures and behaviour. Jesus himself was under no illusion as to the honesty of the religious leaders of the day, publicly uncovering the hypocrisy and mendacity of their apparent piety.

In John 18 we encounter two people who chillingly remind us of human weakness and the continual capacity to deny the truth of a situation as injustice is ignored – Caiaphas and Peter. Caiaphas is perhaps the most tragic, partly because his redemption remains unresolved, unlike Peter who is given another future by Jesus. A terrible thing has happened to this high priest. His loyalty, it seems, lies in the wrong place – not where the truth lies within the life of Christ, a human being who has loved and will bleed, but in obedience to the institution itself. Justice, it seems, has ceased to become relevant, and his loyalty lies in the pleasing of the people.

The choice we usually focus on in this passage is the choice between Jesus and Barabbas. But the choice that is often overlooked and underplayed here is the difference between Jesus and Caiaphas, for Caiaphas can fool us all. His is the voice of sound religion, of an institution we often so easily want to trust but which can be weak and rotten, symbolized in Caiaphas' approach to his problem and his decision to condemn an innocent man. This is not a criticism of Judaism but an example of how human it can be to cling to the safety and rules which any institutional religion can potentially provide.

> The spirit of Caiaphas lives on in every century of religious bureaucrats who confidently condemn good people who have broken bad religious laws. Always for a good reason, of course: for the good of the temple, for the good of the church . . . The deadening spirt of hypocrisy lives on in prelates and politicians who want to look good but not be good.[3]

It lives on, we might add, in all of us who cannot face living with the truth of a situation lest it rock too many boats and we are forced to get out into the water. The theme of Week 4 is *Freedom*, but when we are complicit in untruth or injustice, like Caiaphas, we commit ourselves to bondage rather than liberation. This is precisely the situation Peter finds himself in as he denies any loyalty to his master. His lies slip out so easily. Devastated, he realizes what he has done. And this disciple, who loves Jesus *so* much, who was *so* adamant that it would *not* be him, becomes the denier.

Why does Peter say what he says? If we put ourselves in his shoes (and perhaps we have been there many times?), we begin to understand his reasons. Peter is scared, deeply frightened about what Jesus' fate will be. He has found himself embroiled in a visionary group that, while initially exciting, inviting a new and freeing way of life, now has consequences and commitments that are far graver than he anticipated. After a whirlwind of exhilarating ministry, Peter is suddenly unsure of whether he is ready for the implications of this altered and more costly life. And so he denies the truth, through lies and weakness.

The Bible, like life, is full of incidents of denial and deception. The utter ugliness of human weakness is all there, in the arrogance of the rich young man's question, the proof needed by Thomas, the denial of the unjust judge – and yet this is not the end of the story. For the story finishes in a grace-filled place, as Jesus identifies that

Peter is the one who, surprisingly, holds the capability to build and grow the Church. Although the lies slipped like sand through a sieve, the grains fell to begin to build the base for a resilient future Church, where Peter will be the new good shepherd.

Alan Bennett, in his gently acerbic and insightful way, comments on how many intellectual media institutions and publications communicating 'elegant common sense' so often mask 'a brutal indifference' to anything that truly challenges the status quo.[4] This would be a fitting observation too of Caiaphas' calculated and smooth diplomacy, of doing what is 'right by the people' irrespective of whether justice is truly served.

Peter and Caiaphas are not just historical individuals; they are a universal personification of a weakness that belongs to every person at some stage in life. But time and again in the Gospels and beyond, we witness that God's light can penetrate our cracked humanity, enabling us to discover a new freedom and authenticity which explodes untruth and frees in us a new voice and a new life.

Repentance

The healing of the paralysed man
(Mark 2.1-12)

True repentance brings an urge to be different, because of
the sense of the incessant movement of what I am, forming,
forming, forming what I shall be in the years to come.
(Florence Allshorn, 1887–1950, English missionary, educator
and writer)[1]

My great-great-grandfather was a lesser-known Victorian painter,
Henry Benjamin Roberts. Like many artists of the time he painted
scenes of those who were vulnerable and poor in society and often
those who travelled, including salespeople, gypsies and those who
had no choice but to be itinerant. Many of his paintings, through
ambiguous titles that were popular at the time, describe their immediate subject as well as a moral state or aspiration society should
be striving towards. *Never Too Late to Mend* is one such picture. It
portrays a pure-faced (and rather beautiful) tinker holding up a pot
with a hole in it. The assumption is that old copper pans can always
be mended; the deeper metaphor is, so can humanity.

Repentance is part of the basic message of Jesus. Mark begins
his Gospel with the prophetic, clarion call of John the Baptist
which challenges the people to turn from their sins to begin a new
era; baptism is the outward sign of such commitment for all who
choose this for their lives. Soon afterwards, Jesus walks into Galilee,
preaching a message of repentance and introducing the good news
of God's distinctive kingdom where religious values of the past are
turned on their head.

In many of Jesus' miracles repentance is asked for, as in the healing of the paralysed man in Mark 2. But often repentance is not specifically mentioned (as in the story of Zacchaeus) but it happens anyway, as somehow an encounter with Jesus proves so transformative that it inspires a change of behaviour.

Many biblical texts make connections between illness and sin, and it would be assumed that the reason this particular paralytic has not been granted healing from God over the years is God's disapproval of his past behaviour. Jesus' sweeping statement about forgiveness is scandalous to the traditional teachers of the Law; for them this is a privilege only God can grant.

When Jesus forgives sins, he releases individuals into a renewed and freer existence. Individuals walk away from the prisons of how sin was understood and into a life of newfound flourishing. The paralysed man moves from a physically passive position to a dynamically active one. Repentance, then, is a decisive act, as it moves us from a place of spiritual stagnation to one where we are aware of our own need to change and grow, as the quote from Florence Allshorn suggests.

In our culture of high expectations and anti-institution, modelling public repentance becomes impossible as society demands a 'no-mistake' delivery of every promise and service. Sin has also become a dirty word, with archaic and inappropriate assumptions put upon it. We no longer talk about this specifically as it is associated with damaging and unhelpful morality from weighty and outdated metanarratives. Yet the solitary and writer Maggie Ross brings some balance into this:

Sin matters terribly and matters not at all: matters terribly as a vehicle for evil and matters not at all because it can be transformed in the love of God. Sin, which we cannot avoid, and the acknowledgment of sin, can be a balancing factor, not a morbid preoccupation. It is rather a knowledge that adds reality to the assessment of decisions we are about to make.[2]

She continues by saying that a contemplation of sin can move us from an unhealthy narcissism to understanding that Jesus' message was also a collective one and that the individual healings that he performed were signs of the turning around, the *metanoia*, of the whole world. Yet we cannot deny that responsibility for this begins with us individually (as it does in the Bible), as repentance can become a daily, ongoing practice since it is ever present in our prayers, liturgies, Eucharist and Lord's Prayer.

When Jesus asks people to repent, he is confronting them with the possibility of a radical reorientation of their lives so that they can be freed from all that is hindering their complete wholeness, which is God's intention for everyone. This is why repentance is particularly powerful with individuals who have built up layers of toughness or have begun to believe they are evil or irredeemable.

The Forgiveness Project (2016), compiled by the award-winning journalist Marina Cantacuzino, records stories of forgiveness, reconciliation and conflict transformation. One story records the brutal murder of Bob Hutchinson who, on New Year's Eve in 1997, went to check on a rowdy party being held in a neighbouring house in the small town of Squamish, British Columbia, Canada. Hutchinson was beaten to death in a drug- and alcohol-fuelled attack by a group of young men who objected to his presence there.

After four agonizing years of the authorities trying to find evidence of the perpetrators, Ryan Aldridge finally admitted delivering the fatal blow. When this came to light, Bob's widow Katy wrote to Ryan, asking him to take responsibility for what he had done. Ryan's swift admittance of his crime subsequently led to his transformational remorse and deep repentance. Katy chose to forgive Ryan because she desperately wanted her own life as a mother to be a positive one for her two young daughters rather than one consumed by anger, hatred and grief. Working alongside Ryan at a variety of community speaking events, she has sought to influence the choices others make, trying to prevent further violence and vengeance.

The forgiveness Katy offered Ryan changed his life. Repentance allows people to walk towards a future filled with the air of fresh possibilities and faith, even though pain and guilt may be harder to release.[3]

Jesus understands that the world is a place where people get hurt, where terrible atrocities and injustices happen on a regular basis, where humanity is capable of both unintended as well as deliberate sin and evil. But his concern is always how people respond to their brokenness, what they will do with their mistakes when they happen and their lives when they are bleeding. His desire is to see repentance as active in people's healing and transformation and as a door that is always open.

'"Seventy times seven" is a medicine for a healing community, not for a community with all the answers beforehand and all the appropriate punishments afterwards', says Richard Rohr.[4] Lent is a time when Christians dig deep to commit to practising repentance as an example of continuous self-examination for the world, which allows new possibilities to be born every time we sincerely allow ourselves to act upon it. We become holier through it as the Spirit lifts the weighty armour of sorrow and guilt from our shoulders, and we feel released into becoming potentially more vulnerable yet honest people.

The Christian world view is essentially hope-filled, grace-filled. The acknowledgement and practice of repentance tells us that we are never too late to mend; that however others label us and however dark our histories are as individuals or communities, a new future awaits, set within Christ's patient redemption.

Choice

Peter stepping out of the boat
(Matthew 14.22–33)

Transformed people transform people.
(Richard Rohr)[1]

Each day of our lives presents a surplus of infinitesimal as well as momentous choices. Many of these operate automatically, with habit and necessity all playing their part; in theory we have the possibility to choose anything from the supermarket shelves, but we tend to go for the default option of the food that forms our regular diet. When choice is removed from us, we feel disgruntled, often put out, but when the choices available feel overwhelming, then having less to choose from feels strangely liberating. Choosing can be something we are anticipating or something that we are slowly dreading, depending on what it is.

Two choices are presented to Peter in Matthew 14: to stay in the boat or to get out of it. The boat is, until the storm blows up at least, synonymous with a place of safety, familiarity and friendship. It becomes a metaphor for how we approach the Christian life as we too are invited, often in times of fear and unpredictability, to trust Jesus as we step out of our comfort zone into a new relationship, a new job, a new country or a new stage in our lives, where we somehow understand we are not relying on our strength alone. Peter is brave in this definitive choice, and the text tells us that he only begins to sink when fear and doubt momentarily get the better of him.

Lent is a season in which we are challenged to spend some time thinking about the choices that are available to us as well as the choices that we make. Many Christians live with something of a 'rule of life', a decisive thinking through of how they choose to structure their lives based on the daily rhythm within monastic communities: a basic pattern of prayer, work, service, food and rest. Ideally, every choice we make should be informed by our faith, but perhaps this season provides the opportunity for us to revisit some of the most important questions in this area. How do we use our money, our time and our material possessions (if we have any choice in this)? Who do we choose to spend time with, to listen to, to help?

Jesus' own brief ministry often asks questions of others in terms of the choices they have made as well as the choices they could make. As he heals and liberates those on society's edge, he gives to many new opportunities to fulfil potential or to reorientate lives which can then be fuelled by a different power and a brighter light. As with Peter here, God's underlying vision is to draw all people to a way of life that enables us to be free, primarily free from fear – here even amid the potential danger of drowning.

Richard Rohr, a Franciscan priest and theologian, suggests that as we follow Jesus, the anxiety surrounding some of our choices dissipates as we are continually converted to an understanding that we live as people held and possessed completely in the love of God. This knowledge, if we allow it to change us significantly, can affect every choice we make. Our choices thus become enveloped and infused with looking at each situation automatically and naturally through grace. Rohr says:

> Mature religion involves changing ourselves and letting ourselves be changed by a mysterious encounter with grace, mercy, and forgiveness. This is the truth that will set us free . . . Remember, that it is only transformed people who have the power to transform others, as if by osmosis. Usually you can lead others only as far as you yourselves have gone. In the presence of whole people, or any encounter with Holiness itself, we simply find that after a while, we are different – and much better![2]

Peter is witness to all of this. He experiences the grace, mercy and forgiveness of Christ after the disastrous choices he makes in the

Passion Narrative, as Christ himself chooses to see his potential rather than his weakness. Jesus models the opposite of Peter's choices as he instructs the disciples to fish from the correct side of the boat and as he stands silent before Herod and Pilate, refusing to perjure himself.

The novel *On Chesil Beach* by Ian McEwan and the subsequent film (2017) provide both potential as well as tragic contemplation on choices that have significant consequences. The book is set in the early 1960s, and Florence and Edward are two students from Oxford who have just got married. They spend their honeymoon at a small hotel in Dorset, alongside the stretch of coastline known as Chesil Beach. After a disastrous first attempt at lovemaking, Florence storms out, and the tragedy unfolds on the beach itself, as they say cruel things to each other, and she tells Edward that she will never be interested in the sexual side of a relationship. Edward understandably feels as though significant goal posts have moved, and the couple part company. The Chesil, a physical bank of pebbles between sea and land, becomes a metaphor for the barrier that is created between them.

The novel continues to describe the years that follow for each, but it is not until Edward reaches his sixties that he concludes that, if they had chosen to, he and Florence could have worked things through and enjoyed a happy and fulfilling marriage.

Here as well as throughout the Bible we can conclude that just one choice can have far-reaching consequences. Making hard choices often bears strange fruit: Jesus' own silence condemns him to death but leads eventually to glorious and unequivocal new life for the whole of humanity. Choice is an integral part of the various freedoms we enjoy, and as people of faith, our individual decisions should dovetail with what we interpret to be God's will for the world.

Lent provides the opportunity to review the choices we *have* made, recently as well as historically, as well as the choices we *can* make in the future – maybe there is an important one we have to decide upon currently. As Peter did, we rely on God's discernment to help us with the choices we make, to work peace and healing into the bad choices of the past and to pray for the wisdom to make good choices in the future. We choose how to use our language in a non-violent way, we choose how faith can translate the transformation we have undergone into a renewed and more empathetic approach to others, and we choose the consumer choices we make and the subsequent impact this has on the planet. With this, we can reflect and pray about the lives of those around the globe who are seriously trapped through poverty, lifestyle, sometimes culture, and those who are imprisoned physically or emotionally through a lack of choice.

We are invited to use the choices we enjoy to make inroads into others' lack of it. As people who choose how to live and how to respond to others prayerfully and thoughtfully, we allow God's love to shine through most of the choices we make as we inhabit our freedom in a responsible and grace-filled way.

Prayer and action

- Reflect on the particular 'freedoms' you have in your life, and on those you do not. Are there ways you feel inhibited or trapped in a particular situation, and can you talk or pray about these with someone else? Can you take this further by reflecting on how others in the world have limited freedom in terms of lifestyle choice, faith, speech and political expression as well as career limitations? Is there something you could do as a church to help release new freedom in another's situation?
- Boundaries can be both positive and negative: discuss.
- What boundaries does Jesus disestablish and challenge during his life? Are these detrimental or life-giving to others? How does this mirror how we might approach the concept of boundary in our personal life and our work? Boundaries establish responsibility and protection but can also symbolize a lack of welcome. Where are the boundaries in your own church community? Do some new boundaries need to be created, or others dismantled?
- How do we establish safety in our lives? Do we allow rational or irrational fear to colour how we view the world as well as the choices we make? What are we frightened of, and how could we help others to feel safer in our communities?
- Has there been a time in your life when you have denied something that was true? Can you identify with Peter in this way? How do we feel when we are on the receiving end of denial? Has prayer helped in such a situation, and how is justice connected with denial? Do you know others who are in a state of denial? How can you help them to be honest and truthful about a situation?

- Have there been times in your life when you have felt the need for serious repentance? What did you do? Has this resulted in inner change for you, a feeling of a turning around and a new beginning? How have you experienced this in the life of those you know? Is repentance a process, like forgiveness, or can it happen instantly? What is your experience of confession collectively, in corporate worship?
- Lent is a season when we sometimes consciously limit the choices open to us. Is it hard for us to give things up, and if so, what things would these be? Are these connected with what we consume or how we spend our time? How is limited choice life-giving and how is it life-denying? Is there a way you can support someone else, locally or globally, by opening up more choice for them? For example, by offering to babysit or giving a lift regularly you are potentially providing someone else with more choice.

WEEK 5

Introduction: anxiety

When we feel anxious, we cry out to God (Psalm 107.23–30)

Anxiety

Anxiety is a fiend that sinks its fangs
into my heart, my mind, my soul.
It claws, finding flaws in
All I believe is secure.
It drains my glass of hope
And throws rocks at faith,
Eroding
All my dreams of a future so carefully worked out.
Anxiety is like a heavy cloak
Carrying the weight of that which might never come to pass.
Drenched in so much worrying rain that
It is impossible to continue walking towards the dawn of
New possibilities.
Shut the window. Keep it out.
But anxiety slips through the cracks,
Like the ice-cold wind on a winter's day.[1]

Despite having grown up in the sea-surrounded land of Cornwall, I'm not a fan of deep water. A few years ago, while on holiday, I was out in a small boat on choppy water. Rationally, I knew I was safe, but it took considerable mental effort for me to believe it and to keep my anxiety in check.

There are many passages in the Bible that use the image of a storm at sea to explore the chaos of life and to emphasize a depth of trust in God. The calming of the storm in the Gospel (Luke 8.22–25) has the disciples shouting at Jesus, desperate for him to keep the waves at bay. These few verses from Psalm 107 describe the experience of many who discover the unpredictability of the sea, but they also provide a metaphor for what we might interpret as 'the storms of life'. The verses describe how these merchants who went to sea, initially awed by the immensity of the ocean and the marvels of the deep, soon experienced the volatility of the weather, finding themselves out of control in the midst of a turbulent storm. They quickly lost courage, despite their nautical expertise, having no choice but to cry out to God.

The imagery within these verses is equivalent to how life feels for us at times. We are 'thrown about', bombarded by things that come at us, just as these sailors were drenched by the huge waves that flooded over their boat. Often the things we have to cope with are ongoing and monotonous, but issues can blow up suddenly in our lives just like a squall on the sea. In the biblical text, such 'storms' often indicate two things. First, that often God asks people to step out in courage to do things for him, as he did with Jonah, for example, who desperately didn't want to go Nineveh and found himself in the middle of an exhaustingly watery yet eventually redemptive journey. Or the occasion when Peter found himself battling with the fear of sinking into the water, as a strong wind blew about him after he stepped out from the safety of the boat, yet he eventually mustered the courage to walk on the water towards the Christ he loved and trusted. Second, these passages are often about the reliance on a deep trust in a God who does not necessarily tell us where he is leading us but does reassure us that he will never forsake us, that he is with us always.

These days our lives are complex and sophisticated, which inevitably means there is potentially more to be anxious about. But whether we do, in fact, live in a more anxious age than we did 50 years ago is debatable. It seems more probable that anxiety is and always has been a normal part of life – that people always live with things to worry about. Every historical period brings new challenges in this respect. While we might not live with the unpredictability of a large proportion of young men going off to war or the anxiety of whether our village will be beset with bubonic plague, we live in a time when family breakdown brings all kinds of additional burdens, where jobs are not as secure as perhaps they once were, where so much pressure to succeed is heaped on our younger generation from an early age. We could argue that all of us live with an underlying sense of anxiety running through our lives, like a relentless headache we just can't seem to shift.

If anxiety is to be an inevitable part of life, then perhaps a Christian calling is about learning to transform this positively by living in trust. This chapter offers short reflections on some of the things that prevent us from doing this, things that preoccupy us so much of the time, often creating worry.

Lifestyle is a contemporary concept, one where we receive so many conflicting messages from advertising, which potentially creates pressure for us as we think we must have this or that, that our ways of life must communicate certain messages about who we are. **Money** has traditionally always caused anxiety, whatever income bracket we belong to. The complexity of life fuelled by our technological needs, job insecurity and contentious student loans means that our finances can feel very stretched and we worry about whether 'we can afford it'.

Subjects like this then connect with the underlying **pressure** we feel – for our children to achieve, for us to attain the company's 'targets' in our jobs. Even in our churches we must make sure we increase our numbers and fulfil the feel-good and utopian 'vision statement' or strapline.

Our humanity finds itself struggling in what is essentially part of a beguiling but consumerist wilderness, with pressures that can be hard not to absorb as anxiety mounts through it all. Christ in his own time was no stranger to such pressures either, but offered a way of allowing them to fall off our backs like a too-heavy coat, which the poem at the beginning of the chapter describes.

In the book of Jonah is the constant contrast of Jonah's passivity with God's activity. So often in the Bible, God is seen to invite people out of the lethargy and anxiety that is keeping them right where they are. Moving from wilderness to a grace-filled approach here, there is an encouragement to keep anxiety at bay by an *active* seeking of a replacement energy, a prayerful and decisive intention not to live with anxiety's demanding and exhausting hammerings. We move, therefore, towards a vision where we can be ourselves in **authenticity**, working towards a freedom where we are confident in the people we already are, shaped by a kingdom vision where our individuality is not defined because of what others want us to believe or what we buy or experience, but because we walk each day **trusting** in God's gift of grace.

Lifestyle

Don't make physical existence an anxiety or a fixation
(Matthew 6.25–34)

Ladies and gentlemen, this is Vanity Fair – a world where everyone is striving for that which is not worth having.
(Michael Palin playing William M. Thackeray in ITV's 2018 version of *Vanity Fair*)

Lifestyle is a relatively contemporary concept. We talk of enjoying or sustaining a 'standard of living' these days – something presented as necessary for our emotional and physical well-being. Lifestyle, in this sense, can mean everything from the kind of furniture we have in our homes to the kinds of shops we buy things from to how we spend our time and energy and the kinds of people we like to feel are our friends. Media messages have an impact on what should constitute this 'standard' as well as what we should be aiming for, sending insistent reminders on television and social media of self-sufficiency and stylishness. If the reality of our lives means we cannot enjoy the choice of whether or not to take up such challenges through lack of mobility, funds, education or indeed popularity, then we can find ourselves the victims of an unspoken anxiety. The gospel imperative to live our lives gratefully, joyfully and generously is overlaid with a sense of dissatisfaction and often jealousy of what others have.

In less wealthy societies, 'lifestyle' manifests more in an understood culture of necessity through a simple rhythm of life. Lifestyle is something that is shared, more collective than individual, as opposed to moulded and chosen in a sometimes pretentious and self-conscious way. For centuries, most human beings had no individual understanding of wealth, with the family, tribe or clan taking responsibility for any reserve of resources for times of potential adverse circumstances. As Christian people who follow a first-century man who advocated breathing the freedom of the above verses from Matthew, what should our response be today?

Jesus connects a preoccupation with worrying unduly with the things we all need that connect us all: food, clothes and security for the future. Jesus himself lives a peripatetic life as travelling preacher, healer, nomad and prophet. He enjoys the hospitality of others and, apart from his time with Mary and Joseph, we only have biblical accounts of his residing in the homes of others. Within his own material and symbolic personhood, he models a lifestyle that is free and unencumbered by responsibility. Yet Jesus also enjoys the good things of life. Roland Walls, the founder of the Community of the Transfiguration in Roslin, Scotland, says this:

> Jesus was no ascetic, in the sense that he did not make rules for 'personal mortification'. But he was an ascetic in a more direct and profound way. Jesus had the asceticism of contentment with what was there. When your desires are contained by what is actually there you are rejoicing in your heavenly Father who knows the things you need before you ask for them and being satisfied with the bread that he gives you for the day.[1]

In Jewish culture, the heart was where judgements and decisions were made. In other words, Jesus warns that if we are focused on too much anxiety (for us that means on material possessions, our homes, leisure pursuits or our popularity), then these things will begin to possess us, becoming a form of personal oppression; they will become the hungry gods we worship and which need to be continuously satisfied. Jesus warns his listeners against an inordinate attachment to people, ideas, possessions – indeed, any kind of philosophy that will take our time and energy away from working for God – and encourages us to know that we are children of grace just as we are, without striving for things that are unnecessary.

An overemphasis on all things material prevents us being ready to respond to the needs of the kingdom and robs us of the richness of enjoying the gift of the present moment.

Some years ago, I had some friends I have now sadly lost touch with. Sally and Tom were not wealthy and lived for others, one as a social worker and the other as a community worker. Living in a small terraced house in the south-west, their home was furnished in a beautifully stylish as well as imaginative way. They had a reclaimed pew in the room where they ate. None of their crockery matched, but it was brought together by all being one colour. They stored their dried goods in old sweet jars. Within the house was calm uniformity and style, but nothing was particularly expensive. People of Christian faith, they used their time well and offered a powerful hospitality to friends like me. Many a robust discussion was enjoyed over dinner of fresh, good-quality and well-cooked food. We walked on the hills and went to church in their collective places of worship. Their lifestyle was one that enjoyed the good things of life and was so generously offered to others that it was always a pleasure to spend time with them, though there was the sense that their priorities were always in the right place – to make their guests feel valued and comfortable.

A recent and delightful film, *Finding Your Feet*, centres on the relationship between two sisters. 'Lady' Sandra Abbott has recently discovered that her husband of 40 years has been having an affair with her best friend. Leaving her sprawling house somewhere in the home counties, Sandra lands on the doorstep of her free-spirited and unorthodox sister, Bif. The two could not be more different in either character or lifestyle.

Initially Sandra, with her designer clothes and champagne lifestyle, finds the chaos and shabbiness of Bif's council flat challenging. Yet she finds a new joy and friendship within a very different social network through the dance class that Bif goes along to every week. Dancing mysteriously releases the oppressiveness of the lifestyle Sandra has become locked into and, as the film unfolds, we see her transform her censorious attitudes to her sister's unabashed way of living as she absorbs its inherent spontaneity.

There is authentic joy here even as Sandra discovers that Bif is dying as, rather than shutting life down, this stimulates them both to live life to the full as they travel with their dance group to perform in Rome. By the end of the film, Sandra has also found a new love in Charlie, who has decided to sail to places new in his narrow boat as Sandra comes full circle, shedding the trappings of a static lifestyle to be freer but ultimately happier as she decides to travel with him.

Christianity advocates that each life and all of life, whatever it might bring, is still ultimately a gift, even with the juxtaposition of both joy and pain. To turn the word 'lifestyle' on its head is to understand that we have a choice in how we approach this life. We choose to 'style our lives' as is fitting for those who follow Christ. Our style of life is one where others are invited and included, especially the lonely, the broken and the difficult, where material things are enjoyed but held with a light touch, where experiences are savoured and looked forward to but not hankered unhealthily after, where the present moment is valued and trusted more than the past and within it is an indication of the hope that will open up in a future full of adventurous but worry-free possibility.

Money

Judas betrays Jesus with 30 pieces of silver and then deeply regrets it
(Matthew 26.14-16; 27.3–10)

The use of wealth to acquire security is normal, but it risks
taking us further and further away from being those who wash
feet.
(Justin Welby, Archbishop of Canterbury)[1]

I am writing this reflection on Maundy Thursday, a day when clergy
traditionally wash the feet of members of their congregations, break
bread and share wine – echoes of those sacred and symbolic acts of
service carried out by Jesus in his last few agonized hours. It is the day
when traditionally no money is collected in church services, a sombre
reminder of that ultimate act of betrayal of the shadowy disciple, Judas.

In Matthew's Gospel, Judas goes to the chief priests to ask them
how much they will pay if he tells them exactly where they can find
Jesus in order to arrest him. They give him 30 pieces of silver. Thirty
pieces of silver has resonances in the Old Testament. In Zechariah
11.12 it is the price the prophet receives for his labour, although he
throws it back at the potter, with some scholars connecting this to a
person's actual worth. In Exodus 21.32, the price paid for a slave was
30 pieces of silver. This has overtones of Jesus' own solidarity with
those considered on the bottom rung of society's ladder.

The Bible does not disapprove of money in itself. Individuals
such as Abraham who prosper with the equivalent of wealth in
flocks, herds and agriculture are understood as being blessed by
God. 1 Timothy 6.10 says that it is the *love of money* that is the root

of all kinds of evil. As Justin Welby observes, if we are not careful, Christians often approach the subject with an automatic kind of 'nimby-ish Puritanism', our favourite story of the transformation of miserliness being Scrooge in Dickens's *A Christmas Carol*.[2]

But money is a necessity for most human beings. Whatever our bank balance, money often becomes a worry, an obsession or a regular diversion from 'richer' and more humane things – the experiences that help us to grow and develop as people. Most of us are tempted, often or occasionally, to fantasize about the 'what ifs' of the lottery win or that possible inheritance – a glamorized escape route out of what we perceive to be not enough.

The selling of Jesus by Judas effectively draws together many of money's temptations and associations. On the surface we can only surmise that Judas does what he does because he is lured by greed, through a yearning for some recognition, or possibly because he is frightened of the consequences of being associated with Jesus, and so he jumps ship. But whatever the motive, money here for Judas is not just about the accumulation of wealth; it is also closely connected with power. It changes his status from humble disciple to useful informant, from a nobody to a person who can be called upon by those with religious clout.

Money and power have always gone hand in hand: the more money we have, the more influence and independence we have, on the whole. In the eyes of the world, money builds respect, attention, protection and independence. It buys gated communities, private education and a better standard of living; it buys associations and friendships with particular kinds of people. Yet the selfish accumulation of it, or money's ability to create tight-fisted attitudes, can isolate us from others, and there are plenty of hard-hitting parables in the Bible that warn of the consequences of this. Dives and Lazarus, and the rich but dead man and his vast barns full of decaying crops, are but two. Money and power potentially clothe us in layer upon layer of privilege as we get further and further away from the material needs of others as well as the true vulnerabilities of ourselves.

Money here is also a path to isolation, for it cuts off the relationship Judas has with the community of the disciples, from the person of Jesus and from his participation in the future establishment of God's kingdom. Judas uses money to betray Jesus, as Jesus is now understood as a commodity, which is why this action feels so offensive, because it becomes a symbol of the absolute antithesis of everything Jesus has stood for. Jesus' ministry with and for others has been one of soothing the inner and outer wounds of the ignored, the scarred, the desperate and the poor, as he has noticed and restored many individuals who could so easily have been dispensed with.

Redemption comes perhaps with Judas' remorse in chapter 27 as, in a light-bulb flash of repentance, he tries to reverse his actions and return the money, but it is too late.

Ghislaine Howard has painted a powerful painting called *Judas – The Departure*. It depicts Judas putting on a dark coat. The image is both ordinary as well as monumental in its overtones: it could simply be a man going out to do something he does every day, or it could be that here is someone caught up, trapped in an act of vast and cosmic consequence. When the painting was displayed in York Minister in 2011, the then Dean, Keith Jones, offered some reflections. He described the figure as possessing a monumental grandeur as well as a tragic sadness, as a man who reminds us of so many who are pulled and tugged by money, wealth, power and status, and of how all these things can insidiously take hold of us. Jones saw resonances of those we continuously read about in the newspapers or hear about on social media: the bankers, politicians and celebrities as well as sometimes ourselves, those who are tempted by money's siren call, who have fallen from grace, those who:

> look like the masters of the world but who, of course, are also prisoners . . . of what has gone before, formed [by] the situations in which they exercise their limited choices . . . He represents a man trapped by his own self-confidence and convictions: the aspects of our society that have won us astonishing triumphs of technology and mastery, but at the cost perhaps of what Jesus called the one thing needful. 'What does it profit a man to gain the whole world at the cost of his life?'[3]

Money is necessity, but it is to be kept in perspective – always. Sometimes it buys the wrong things, such as friendship and intimacy, states of existence that should ultimately never be bought. We need to heed its potential to become a personal and political idol, for it is an easy pathway into very dark ways of behaviour which can make prisoners of us all, wildernesses that create jealousy and eternal dissatisfaction with our lot. Yet correctly approached and used, along with a grace-filled understanding that it is always a gift as well as simply a means to an end, money is a tool to buy good and necessary things and enables us to experience the joy of life, to establish relationships and community and to communicate the continual abundance of God.

Pressure

Pressure is put on Peter to be honest about his affiliation with Jesus
(Mark 14.66–72)

God is acting on your soul all the time, whether you have
spiritual sensations or not.
(Evelyn Underhill, 1875–1941)[1]

Peter, wrapped in gloom and shadows, sitting by the fire in the temple courtyard, is perhaps one of the most evocative images in the Passion Narrative.

The confused disciples scatter after Jesus' arrest; they do not lack courage or character in doing so, for this is a natural reaction. This fleeing is the result of their faith being shaken to its very foundations. Peter himself wants to slip into anonymity to catch his breath and clear his head, to come to terms with the fact that, despite living alongside Jesus and witnessing his divine power for months, this extraordinary man has decided not to save his own skin. He shows no resistance to his enemies; the only weapons used are the silence of justice and the truth as, through them, Jesus exposes all that is mendacious and cruel.

Contrasted to such integrity, the denial of Peter is a real and serious fall from grace, what feels like an unforgivable disloyalty. But Peter is frightened, and he understands what happens to crazy rebels who dare to challenge the status quo of the Roman regime or of the religious power groups who are so often their obsequious supporters.

Peter could be any one of us as we ask ourselves the question, 'What would *we* have done in such a situation?' Can we really be loyal to what or who we say are important to us? And we believe

Peter when he adamantly tells his master at the Last Supper that he will *not* abandon him (Mark 14.29). How many times has this been us too – when we have promised the world and then run away, unable to stay loyal to a task or role that is simply too great?

Here in this courtyard, the only comfort is from the warmth of the spitting embers, and Peter feels the mounting pressure as people begin to recognize him, begin to make the connections with his Galilean origins and his association with Jesus. His mind is on overdrive – there may be a witch-hunt seeking to gather up all who are associated with Jesus. He sees before him the prospect of a violent and agonizing death, imprisonment, torture, and it terrifies him.

As the disciples disperse, they begin to lose, at least temporarily, the sense of community that has formed over the last few years of living alongside Jesus as his closest companions; it is much harder to resist pressure without the support of others.

Something of these feelings of being frozen with fear, of self-protection and of insistent pressure has some reverberations with those who are witnesses to unpredictable mass shootings the world over. The USA has suffered a great deal in this respect. The latest incident at the time of writing unfolded at Marjory Stoneman Douglas High School in Parkland, Florida, when Nikolas Cruz, armed with an AR-15 rifle, entered the school and launched an attack. Seventeen children and adults died in this terrible episode, and it was subsequently discovered that Cruz was a former expelled pupil who had been suffering from poor mental health. On 21 February 2018, *The Guardian* reported the incident as the eighth deadliest mass shooting in contemporary US history, the second greatest loss of life since the 2012 massacre at Sandy Hook elementary school in Newtown, Connecticut. In 2018, there were at least eight school shootings in the USA.[2]

This led to a rally of thousands of young people in Washington on 24 March 2018 to pressure the government to repeal the legislation on the possession of arms and to stand up against influential collectives such as the NRA (National Rifle Association), which is hugely influential in the USA. Several young people spoke with passion and conviction, themselves the family members or friends of some of the victims of past gun crimes. Seventeen-year-old Edna Chavez, who lost a brother to gun violence, said that she had learnt to duck from bullets before she learned to read. The great granddaughter of Martin Luther King, Yolanda Renee King, said, 'I have a dream that enough is enough. And that this should be a gun-free world, period.' Barack and Michelle Obama tweeted that the marchers were an inspiration.[3]

The rally stimulated more than 830 marches worldwide and put pressure on Congress to tighten the country's notoriously relaxed approach to firearms, even though there may be a long way to go.

This emotional yet focused rally is the opposite of pressure that seeks to incapacitate people through fear or panic, as it inspires individuals to join together to stimulate genuine and significant change. Pressure builds strength of public opinion until those who are pressurized have no choice but to at least take notice and listen.

Pressure of popularity became the perceived threat to the status quo for Jesus, and then flipped over to his disadvantage with the venom of the mob as, in the end, it bayed for his downfall. Pressure that is honourable in its cause is usually influential and can, with the motives of God's kingdom, change the world. It was international pressure that eventually brought apartheid to its knees, pressure that formulated Vatican II, pressure that resulted in a global ban on nuclear weapons testing (the first campaign launched by Greenpeace in 1971). It is pressure that witnesses school students striking from school to press for more speed within the global climate-change agenda.

Pressure is equivalent to the continuous pounding of a spiritual heartbeat; it carries a conscience and invites a conscientization. Peter feels the excruciating personal pressure to be loyal to Jesus in those agonizing moments after his arrest, the pressure to loyally *not* deny the man who has inspired all the disciples to live their lives with a raw new meaning and purpose which could potentially paint the world with new colour and life. He knows instantly that he has done the wrong thing, yet strangely, even after his denial, more pressure comes in the post-resurrection encounter with Jesus as he is challenged again to adhere and advocate for his newfound faith discovered through Christ. Within the wilderness of human weakness and failure appears an irrefutable belief that here is a second chance for Peter to begin to build the Church and to be a witness to the dawning of a new era for the world.

Authenticity

Palm Sunday
(Mark 11.1–11)

Nowadays I like hotels, at any rate in small doses; they're a setting where you see people trying to behave, which is always more interesting than them just behaving. When people are on their best behaviour they are not always at their best.
(Alan Bennett)[1]

It remains difficult for us to construct a finely honed character analysis of Jesus Christ from the Gospel narratives. At various points he shows emotion; there are hints that he is fond of particular people. He must be kind because we know his heart goes out to the lost-sheep crowds; we know he gets tired, because he escapes the ferocious demands of those who seek him out as the radical new prophet on the block; we know he gets angry, as he storms the temple which has become so sullied with selfish and corrupt practices. But whatever Myers–Briggs type Jesus might be, we can rest assured that he is, throughout his recorded ministry, unashamedly and authentically himself – no face, no mask, no phony persona, no keeping up appearances.

But Jesus works hard too to reject the impression that others have of him. At points in the Gospels he challenges the disciples and others to tell him who they think he is as he asks, 'Who do people say that I am?' (Matthew 16.13–20).

In a world obsessed with popularity, fame, power and money – the old chestnuts of human attainment – there is still a sense that often people can recognize authenticity when they find it. When we reach Palm Sunday, Jesus has worked hard at batting away the inherited perception the Jewish people carry – that the promised and imminent Messiah would arrive in military splendour and majesty, astride a powerful stallion, to release the people from the oppression of the current age. But by now, many of them have listened carefully to the subversion of this strange preacher, as he has turned upside down the values of the age with a different vision.

The people lay their cloaks on the road – an extraordinary act considering they would be ridden over by the humblest of beasts, a colt. Matthew and Mark's Gospels describe the people waving branches (in John they are specifically palms) from the nearby trees. Like a country's flag today, the palm branch was the symbol of Jewish national identity. By waving palms and ushering Jesus into the city that would eventually kill him, the people are affirming Jesus as their leader, their king. His 'triumphal entry' is a statement of belief, of trust, of recognition that, however it might happen, there is the expectation that this man will overturn the systems of oppression they feel trapped within. This very public procession causes great upset and unease for the Sanhedrin and Roman rulers and is the beginning of the end for Jesus.

Most of us live wearing different masks and inhabiting a multitude of different personas depending on the roles and tasks that our lives demand. This is normal and natural and illustrates the complexity of life. We struggle with our hang-ups, people pleasing, living behind thin walls of formality or even dishonesty. We know that it is mostly those we are closest to, those whom we truly trust, who see us naked in the fragility, rawness and sometimes ugliness we are capable of and which we mostly try to keep contained. This is why Jesus remains so adamant that it is children who are the signposts and inheritors of the kingdom, for it is children who are so good at all of this. What you see is usually what you get, as they call a spade a spade and ask the questions we shy away from or have become frightened to answer as adults.

When we meet authenticity, it challenges us, for it cuts through all untruth and all falseness. People who are particularly good at this are kingdom people, those who have nothing much to lose, those who are pure in heart, those who are natural, those who have no 'face' and who are content and secure simply being who they are without striving to be anything that they are not.

Authenticity is often prevented by low self-esteem, which sometimes results in antisocial behaviour, addiction or a dangerous searching for identity in the belonging associated with gang culture. Or authenticity cultivates a kind of shrugging-off of gracious behaviour or improvement – this is simply 'me' with no sense that there is or should be room for improvement or compromise in terms of the consideration of others. We must be careful with this as people of faith, for we exist within a metanarrative that allows us to understand ourselves as sinful and flawed, and to celebrate the fact that we can exist in a judgement-free community where everyone is welcomed and idiosyncrasies are celebrated. But within this should lie a natural compass point that draws us back to an understanding that we are nevertheless always striving to be renewed and redeemed people, working for a deep transformation of ourselves. This is where our authenticity and confidence to 'be ourselves' should reside – in the knowledge that we are loved and valued by Jesus and that we are always 'works in progress'.

The writer and playwright Alan Bennett has the piercing ability to observe life through its many subtle layers and peculiarities, as the quote at the beginning of this chapter evidences. His descriptions of people and situations fuse with a gentle poignancy and keen honesty which cut through much of the societal and expected nonsense we so often feel compelled to play to through etiquette and niceness.

Reflecting on his parents, Bennett understands both his mother and his father as people trapped within their own perceptions of themselves, a fact that kept them prisoners to a certain way of living their lives:

The real solvent of class distinction is a proper measure of self-esteem, a kind of unselfconsciousness. Some people are at ease with themselves, so the world is at ease with them. My parents thought this kind of ease was produced by education: 'Your dad and me can't mix; we've not been educated'. They didn't see that what disqualified them was temperament, just as, though educated up to the hilt, it disqualifies me. What keeps us in our place is embarrassment.[2]

Bennett enjoys writing about people who have no sides to them, individuals who are often understood as quirky or gloomy failures but who, because of their authenticity, their lack of pretence and their inexorable approach to life, become interesting – figures like Miss Shepherd and the writer and poet Philip Larkin, on whom Bennett has reflected throughout his literary career.

Jesus rides into Jerusalem having embraced the ministry he has been living and, as he does, his itinerant-prophet persona becomes incorporated into the more divinely mystical position as God's Son. He shrugs off the mighty Messiah that so many are expecting him to accept, the valued and expected image of the age. Here a past life becomes fused with the present, which leads inextricably into a new future, driven by the love and sacrifice of the cross, his life moving far beyond his own individuality to become a symbol for all people across time and space.

As the people of God, we are beautifully complex and wondrously made, often prisoners of a past and an individuality we are not at peace with. But we are eternally in a state of becoming. We cannot live the excuse that says we should remain trapped in a self-absorption and easy acceptance that tells us this is 'just who I am'; rather, we can energize and centre ourselves on what is most important to us – on Christ, who walks gently forward with us into the future.

Trust

Jesus tells his listeners not to lose heart and promises his presence through the Holy Spirit (John 14.1–4, 18–28)

Boundless is thy love for me,
Boundless then my trust shall be
(Robert Bridges, 1844–1930)[1]

Through the wilderness anxieties of money, lifestyle and pressure, trust becomes the element that converts them all. Living in trust enables us to view and approach any uncertain or unknown situation with a faith-based attitude, providing our souls with the breathing space necessary for living our lives at a hope-filled altitude.

We live most of our lives trusting in others: we trust the pilot of the aircraft we fly in, we trust that the water flowing from our taps is clean, we trust that our children are safe with those who care for them, and we trust that many with specific professional expertise have our best interests at heart. Subconsciously we trust, for if we stop to think about how much our life is held in others' hands we might not sleep at night.

Entrusting our lives to the living God holds a more decisive and powerful energy. Jesus models this as he nears the end of his life. He tells his disciples to trust in God and not to be anxious as he begins to build their confidence as the people who will continue the message and ministry that he has begun. His disciples have not seen God, but they now know *of* God because they have experienced Jesus. They will not be left alone after their leader is gone but will be sent a helper – the Holy Spirit of God – who will help them discern the life of love active in the world. Therefore, trust is relational because Jesus connects this to both his Father and the Holy Spirit. This relates to our own experience too, as we learn to trust those who have provided an honest and consistent presence in our lives.

In the final verses of chapter 14, Jesus reiterates again that his friends are categorically not to be troubled, that his parting gift to them is *peace*, a peace that is deeper, a peace of substance which will be a tool for them to draw upon even in times of hardship and suffering.

Yet in our own society there is a strong sense of a disappearing trust in the great institutions of our age, be it the European Union, the established Church, the police, and sometimes the legal system and the NHS. Trust is often held in a fine balance, even within our closest relationships, as we sometimes rely on the wisdom of another to enable us to trust, particularly if this relates to something in the future. The image of trapeze artists is a powerful one as it involves the trust of the acrobats – both the one who is catching and the one who has to time his or her leap at exactly the right moment. This cannot happen without an intimate knowledge of each other's timing and skill as both work in harmony. To trust in this way entails endless practice, and perhaps many falls and bruises along the way.

Living and acting in trust is the opposite of living life in anxiety. It is a recalibrating of the approach we take to any situation. Rather than worrying about what job I might have next year, it is asking, 'Lord, bring me peace of mind even if the opportunities haven't arisen yet.' Rather than being anxious about whether the operation will go well, we put our trust in the expertise of the surgeon and the highly sophisticated medical advancements of our time. Rather than worrying about whether our children's birthday party will be acceptable to other parents, we remember that it is really about the joy of celebrating our own child's landmarks and being grateful for the opportunity to do so.

As people of faith we have the choice as to how we view any situation. Do we close something down because of anxiety or do we tune into the frequencies of the Spirit, who leads us ever onwards in a trustful adventure?

St Teresa of Avila spent a long time deciding whether the religious life was a commitment she could make. When she did decide to enter holy orders, the decision felt as natural as breathing, and her contributions to ascetics have reaped great rewards for many people over the centuries. Her spirituality is punctuated with a sense of deep trust in God and a belief that followers of Christ should trust that God puts us exactly where we are meant to be at any given time.

I am a great fan of the adventure writer and traveller Levison Wood. Wood has travelled the world, often on lengthy walks. He has walked the length of the River Nile, traversed a route through the Himalayas and hiked through Central America. One of his first journeys as a young man was travelling the Silk Road from Russia through the dangerous lands of the Caucasus Mountains to the exotic spice lands of India. He is a man with an innate sense of adventure and an insatiable curiosity about the colourful cultures he discovers, and the risks he takes sometimes feel immense as well as reckless. In his book *Eastern Horizons: Hitchhiking the Silk Road* (a record of this latter journey), he regularly ends up in remote, often inaccessible villages with very little in the way of money or plans for the next stage of his journey. Wood's approach to his life and travels arises from a sense of unadulterated adventure coupled with generous doses of awe, gratitude and resilience, which means that trusting that all will be well simply becomes a natural and inevitable part of his journeying.

Primarily we are asked to live our own lives in trust because, as the opening quote suggests, we live in the knowledge that we are *loved* by God, that God wants, yearns for the best for us. Richard Rohr, a Franciscan writer and mystic says, 'Jesus praised faith and trust even more than love. It takes a foundational trust to fall or to fail – and not to fall apart.'[2] In other words, to live a life in trust is not to say that life will run easily or smoothly but that somehow all is held in the ultimate care of God.

Trust is not a blind and foolish abdication of taking life into our own hands decisively. It is more a courageous and daily living out of the belief that, within unpredictability, trust can lead us on to fresh perspectives as well.

Prayer and action

- As an individual and as a church, how can you help someone who is overcome by anxiety? Don't forget that anxiety can be caused by a variety of different things, including insecurity, bullying, hunger, lack of funds, loneliness.
- Is money an emotive subject for you? How could you change your attitude towards your finances? Is there a good balance between spending and what you spend your money on, between being generous and being careful with regard to the future? Is there someone specific whom you could help support this Lent and maybe beyond?
- Are you conscious of living in or with a particular lifestyle? What kinds of messages does your home communicate to those who come into it? Is your own lifestyle something you enjoy, or has it become a burden? What kinds of messages do you think you communicate through your particular lifestyle? As a Christian, how could you model a healthy lifestyle in terms of your home, your possessions, the ways you spend your time? Who have you met who has impressed you with a different (maybe more natural and freer) way of life?
- As a church community, how could you promote and encourage a sustainable, joyful, balanced and generous approach to living your life?
- Where are the pressures in your own life? In the life of your church?
- How could you (and others) use pressure as a catalyst for change? What about as a church? Is pressure being put on you or your community in a negative way?

- Who are the people in your life who are most able to 'be themselves' without putting on a front or mask? How do they have an impact on others, both positively and negatively? How is God asking *you* to be more authentic in terms of who you are?
- What areas in your life need more trust injected into them? How can you trust God more? And how can you encourage others to trust God more?

WEEK 6

Introduction: pain

Jesus carries his cross to Golgotha (John 19.17–24)

Pain
She runs to gather her up,
Holding her tight.
This little girl is hurt
With grazes and shock.
She has fallen off the swing.
Anguish absorbed in a maternal body
Of warmth and understanding.
She will not let go
Until all is calm,
A reverence is restored and
A knowledge
That this is how divine love always is.[1]

The vicar of a challenging neighbourhood, Sam Wells, in his recent book *Face to Face*, describes a time when a group of teenage lads surprised him with their response to pain. One late summer's afternoon this group knocked on his door, bringing a shoebox with a wounded blackbird in it. The bird, which the boys had found nearby, had a damaged wing and a crooked leg. He says:

> In a community where a lot of people had thrown stones at the church it was quite a moment. I realized all I was being asked to do was to touch and stroke the bird and to affirm the boys in their compassion. Eventually we all went to the vet together.

> But the most important thing was to receive that bird as a gift brought forward in an unwitting offertory procession; for me to turn that offering into a prayer.[2]

Within this exquisite snapshot of the unpredictability of parish life is evidence that most people are attuned and sensitive to pain. Sometimes this arrives unexpectedly in life, as it did for Wells, as well as often being a more continuous presence. Pain is mysteriously unique – no one can experience what we ourselves go through even if it might be similar to that of someone else. Alternatively, many wilderness experiences are of collective pain, which are communal and shared – not that this makes them any easier to bear. Pain is emotional and physical, acute as well as a dull ache of long-term conditions of illness as well as existence.

In the Bible, pain is exemplified in the lament of the psalmists' voices as they rail against the loss of the presence of God, personal security and national identity. In our own age we often react to pain's immediate impact but seem less able to identify and face its roots. We suppress such pain so often, with inappropriate use of medicine as well as resorting to unhealthy approaches to our appetites.

As Christians we are encouraged to share and absorb one another's pain, in whatever measure, for pain is always linked to love. The poem above describes the simple and instinctive sharing by a mother of a young child's pain as she falls from a swing. As she does so, the anguish of the child becomes carried within her own person and is shared through her own response. Such a response is often repetitive as we listen over and over again and support those who we are close to or have responsibility for.

Jesus lives this dynamic out too, as he listens and responds to the suffering of long-term illness, death, isolation, physical disability and many painful conditions. He notices and takes seriously those who have become separated from mainstream society, he hears the anguish of those who are desperate, and he experiences his own extreme physical pain through a brutal death on the cross. In his incarnated life, he demonstrates that all of us, including God, are vulnerable.

Our inhabited bodies are capable of extraordinary healing as well as being strangely unpredictable. When we are in pain, we may feel abandoned, as Jesus did on the cross, yet the Bible constantly re-assures us that God is with us when we suffer. At no point in human history has God, in his love, not shared or grieved over our pain.

Some pain in our lives is necessary – whether physical or emotional – because it communicates to us that something has become dysfunctional and needs attention. It also often moves us into a new place within our lives. The American theologian Matthew Fox offers a powerful image of dealing with pain from the Japanese poet Kenji Miyazawa: 'We must embrace pain and burn it as fuel for our journey.'[3] The image is of a bundle of sticks that is picked up and carried over to a fire, burnt to be dispensed with but which then provides a new energy and focus for the next stage of life. In the sense of pain being an ongoing condition, such a process needs to be exercised daily.

The Boy Who Harnessed the Wind is the true story and 2019 film directed by Chiwetel Ejiofor about William Kamkwamba, a young boy in Malawi with a flair for engineering. Owing to climate change and general poverty, the corn harvest of his community fails. Many slide into frightening poverty and his own family are robbed of the little food they have, and William's sister leaves for a better life. But William has a passion for salvaging electronic components from the local tip because he believes he can create a wind turbine that could provide a vital and continuous source of irrigation for the local crops. William's father, Trywell, is portrayed as a desperate man and one who, until the last part of the film, refuses to grasp his son's vision for the project.

The film feels bleak and full of pain until Trywell begins to trust his son, giving up the family bicycle to provide essential compo-nents to make the turbine. The story describes how hope emerges from pain and how vision is possible even in an apparently despair-ing and resigned situation.

Engaging with pain and being involved in another's experience needs sustained care, which is hard if we are not directly involved. It takes a brave pilgrim to visit Auschwitz. As Walter Brueggemann says in *The Prophetic Imagination*, in the Church there is the need not only for lament but also for vision and memory[4] – we must continue to *see* as well as share our own and others' pain, from the past as well as within the present, for it is vital we do not forget what such an experience does to us as people.

Aspects of **pain** that we reflect upon in this chapter are those which make connections with Jesus' ministry as well as his final hours. Great harm was caused to his embodied humanity through the **weakness** of several individuals. When **dislocation** happens in an individual or within a community, pain arises, often because unresolved pain has created the dislocation in the first place. **Desolation** is pain at its deepest and darkest level, the accusation of absolute abandonment from the cross, and **prejudice** provides a voice for what so many suffer still in the world today. **Waiting** is perhaps subtler, but a part of the Easter story nevertheless, manifest in the loss and frustration of the pause of Holy Saturday and the irresolution of an event such as the fire at Grenfell Tower.

The themes within this chapter are ones where we perhaps need to find the courage to stay in the wilderness for a little while. Grace will be found in the final reflections after the glorious surprise of Easter Sunday.

Weakness

Jesus before Pilate
(John 18.19—19.42)

Is life so wretched? Isn't it rather your hands which are too
small, your vision which is muddied? You are the one who
must grow up.
(Dag Hammarskjöld, 1905–61)[1]

There is nothing worse than weak leadership. Ineffectiveness, not
grasping the bull by the horns, manipulation and procrastination
can all be signs of such weakness. I recognize this in my own life
– times when I have made friends with someone for the wrong reasons because I thought they would be useful, occasions when I have
allowed someone to remain in a role in church because I couldn't
face the fight it would take to remove them, or times when I have
not done the right thing because I didn't want to face the consequences of speaking out or standing alone.

Weak leadership comes in many forms. My daughter, usually a
generous and amenable girl, always returns to one of the rare times
in her school history when she stood up to a teacher because she believed the teacher was offering hypocritical leadership. This teacher
had asked her to take her earrings out (banned for sensible reasons
when playing sport). 'That's fine, Miss', she said. 'I'll take my earrings
out if you take all of yours out too.' In her mind, the teacher should
have led by example. Predictably, the teacher saw red but, understanding my daughter's sense of justice, I could see what she meant.

It's easy to vilify characters like Pilate or Judas, until the dawning
realization comes that we have been exactly like that on occasions

too. Pilate is a man who knows what the truth is but does not want to take responsibility, so instead he negates it all by the archetypical washing of his hands. Yet Pilate does try – he understands publicly what the crowd wants, and he states several times that this is not fair, that this is not a situation of justice or of kindness. But he is on a losing wicket. The crowd includes both venomous religious leaders and ordinary people, gathered in the forum for the prefect's decision at this year's Passover time – to release one prisoner and to send another to his doom. His confidants are successfully swaying the opinion of the crowd and of the decision-maker, so that any compassion is flowing quietly away down the proverbial plughole.

We do not know whether Jesus believes his arrest to be inevitable or not, a consequence of his own mission or a duty he feels bound to because of his Father's will for all of history and humankind. In the final chapters of the Gospels, Jesus undergoes two trials – one religious, the other political. He appears before two courts, the first of which is the Sanhedrin (the Supreme Council of the Jews), where he is accused of blasphemy. Then, later, he is brought before the Roman Governor, Pilate, accused of being a political agitator.

The reason for this double process is that the Jews, under Roman rule, have lost the power to issue the death sentence. After judging Jesus according to Mosaic law, they ask Pilate to effectively sign his death warrant. Pilate procrastinates because he recognizes that Jesus has done nothing wrong, other than stirring up ordinary people in empowerment through a new vision of non-oppression.

Jesus' trial and condemnation to death are not very different from what happens to many Christian militants and martyrs the world over. Undertaking such a ministry and existence does not constitute a crime in any society, but it is often enough to bring persecution to many brave individuals.

We are reflecting on weakness in the week in which pain is the overarching theme. Living in the light enables us to keep perceiving what the truth is in any given situation, even if this takes discernment and discipline and, as here, untangling an emotional and unfair situation. There are different levels of truth that exist in any one situation. Here, Jesus as 'king' is not understood as a military threat to people like Pilate, but he is a threat nevertheless because the vision he brings and the way he lives and responds makes him the popular warrior-king and champion of the poor. His humanity as well as his divinity threaten the status quo.

On 5 October 2010, at the Conservative Party Conference hosted in Birmingham, a deputy head teacher from an inner London school made a passionate speech which can still be viewed on YouTube.[2] From her experience of teaching in five different schools, Katharine Birbalsingh advocated that, through the well-meaning policies of white, liberal politicians, the state education system was keeping black and poor children in a perpetual state of underachievement. She convincingly argued that the current policies had produced a culture of low expectations of achievement, coupled with disciplinary leniency and a decline in educational standards.

The speech, because of its searing, heart-of-the-matter truth, cost Katharine her job. Afterwards, she had hundreds of emails from other teachers around the country who told her they were encountering similar dynamics in achievement for poor and ethnic-minority pupils but were terrified to speak out lest they became branded as troublemakers. Katharine's vision continues to be one where *all* children, regardless of background, class and finances, are well disciplined and where high expectations are assumed; this, she believes, is the secret to young people achieving much. She went on to found her own independent state school, the Michaela Community School, and to influence several others. Katharine's is a sometimes controversial yet single-minded vision of believing that the best can be open to all people. Her motto is 'Success is never final, failure is never fatal, it's courage that counts.'

Although hyperbole is clearly something she thrives on, her motives are honourable and her courage admirable. She has received death threats and has been vilified in the press and by others in the education system but has stuck to her guns in terms of the principles with which she runs her school, and through it all she continues to be an inspiration to others.[3]

Pilate, too, is someone who already enjoys a platform of responsibility and status. The difference is that he chooses to remain sitting on his cushioned throne of complacent privilege – refusing to challenge or expose the lies in the hearts of those who state that Jesus is a rebel troublemaker who needs to be disposed of. Preferring to wear the cloak of lies and easy falsehood because the fight is simply too great, he panders to the vitriol and viciousness of the crowd, who want to see blood. Beaten down by surreptitious efforts to release Jesus quietly, Pilate simply gives in. He leaves the situation strangely tainted and his integrity deeply challenged by another who is much braver than he. Jesus is left in painful and dangerous isolation as he begins his walk to his death.

Dislocation

The crucifixion of Jesus
(Matthew 27.32–44)

Something is rotten in the state of Denmark.
(William Shakespeare, *Hamlet*)[1]

On Sunday night television a familiar scene unfolds. As a crime drama draws to its conclusion, the wrong person is in the investigation room being grilled by our favourite detective, whoever that may be. But there's half an hour to go, so as viewers we work out that it can't possibly be the person in the chair.

Jesus finds himself drawn into a similar scenario of threat, but the conclusion to his interrogation is not to be one of misunderstanding or release, but something far darker. In this final chapter of his life, he is out of sorts, betrayed by the masses who claimed to love him, by the religious authorities and by his closest friends. Soon he will find himself surrounded by unscrupulous individuals who care nothing for his future. He is living, travelling through these final hours, but he is dislocated from everything he has been a part of – the rural Galilean community, his family and his close circle of friends. He is existing, but this is all it is, waiting for the trajectory that is his alone to envelop him like a surging wave, hoping that God and others playing their role in the drama will accelerate his inevitable trial and the eventual resolution of this terrible time.

When we arrive in a foreign city, disorientation happens. Sights, smells, sounds and people appear different from normal.

We may involve ourselves in familiar things – walking, eating, sleeping – but it somehow doesn't feel like the world we usually inhabit. Jerusalem is like this for Jesus now – a dreamlike, film-set atmosphere.

As Jesus is thrown out with his cross thrust upon him, he stumbles – the Stations of the Cross liturgy tells us this happens three times – as he walks himself to his chilling place of death. On this journey there is both disregard as well as kindness. Simon of Cyrene relieves Jesus' suffering by having the cross foisted upon him, but carries it nevertheless. The legend of Veronica has this unknown woman wiping Christ's face with a cloth. Even amid dislocation, it seems that God brings allies.

But harsher voices invade too: the people along the way are disappointed that Jesus has been reduced to this, the religious leaders are relieved that he will soon no longer prove to be a threat, and one of the bandits crucified alongside Jesus makes derogatory remarks. It is a terrible thing that this city, the capital of the Jewish nation, is a place where Jesus is no longer at home.

An immensely powerful film, *Three Billboards outside Ebbing, Missouri*, was screened in UK cinemas in 2018. It is the story of a woman who, although living in her home town of Ebbing, has become dislocated from its people and culture. Mildred Hayes is angry, and her anger is so intense and vengeful that it does not care about the aftermath of violence it leaves in its wake. The reason is that her daughter, Angel, was raped and brutally murdered months ago, yet still the killer has not been found. Mildred creatively highlights this failure by using three decaying billboards on the edge of the town to advertise the fact that, in her opinion, the local police have been useless. The focus of her venting is the town's popular chief of police, William Willoughby.

Mildred attempts to expose what she believes to be institutional incompetence coupled with a sense of lackadaisical justice, and her defiant and unsentimental behaviour rattles the cages of the conservative townsfolk, who all hold Chief Willoughby in high regard. Yet Mildred remains purposeful and focused on getting justice for her daughter, and it is an irrelevance to her that Willoughby is in the final stages of cancer. Through her actions she creates difficulties for her remaining son, best friend and ex-husband and those who try to help her as she becomes more and more isolated through her desperation, anger and grief, all of which are slowly worked out, perhaps redeemed, by the film's conclusion.

Three Billboards is a film about how a broken woman, whose motives are basically good, becomes dislocated from her own community. Mildred's unapologetic yearning for the truth to out is impressive to watch, however much those viewing might disagree with how she goes about it. Neither she nor Dixon (Willoughby's second in command, and bad-egg cop) cease to behave offensively until Willoughby, unable to bear the indignity as his cancer progresses, takes his own life. In letters from the grave, Willoughby challenges both Dixon and Mildred to see their situations and indeed their futures in a more positive, loving and forgiving way. Although more violence follows, with Mildred petrol-bombing the police station and Dixon beating up the local journalist, eventually their rage begins to dissipate as Dixon himself takes on Mildred's case. Slowly a depth of inner transformation begins to happen, shifting all that is not right as both characters join forces to face a new and potentially redemptive future.

In some ways, the film contains resonances with the last stages of Jesus' life and ascent to the cross – how weakness, lazy justice and anger can become a vicious circle, even indulgent; a dynamic that is unable to shift without a new humility and the grace of God.

Dislocation in its many forms is a wilderness experience for many in the world. The dislocation of a limb does not tally with a healthy, happy body or community. It is an experience that keeps others potentially marooned, separated from a community that considers itself 'normal' and calibrates the status quo.

Jesus is killed outside the city of Jerusalem. Mildred's bill-boards of truth are outside her town. In Mildred's life as well as in

Jesus' own, all of this is eventually recognized and transformed, with anger burned out or absorbed, to miraculously open up a new future.

Desolation

The cry of Jesus from the cross
(Mark 15.33–39)

Keep your heart in peace; let nothing in this world disturb it:
everything has an end.
(John of the Cross, 1542–91)[1]

The guttural scream from the cross comes from the absolute depths
of Jesus' humanity: 'My God, my God, why have you forsaken me?'
That fact alone – that Jesus screams – is a shocking and scandalous
thing, for there is a part in all of us that understands God as the
one in control, composed and confident in his omnipotent person
and mission. Now, here is Jesus as God, the one who has powerfully
released others, yet we see him at his lowest point where everything
is flung to the wind and all control is lost as he lies naked and bloodied, pinned by cruel nails to a cross that he cannot escape.

The first person singular – '*My* God' – makes this doubly terrible. This is the same sentiment as one of our own children crying
out to us, demanding to know why they have been made to suffer
so dreadfully. Throughout his ministry, Jesus has had the powerful sense of God being his Father. Effectively, he now cries out in
despair, 'Why has this happened to *me*, that I have to endure such
physical and spiritual pain?'

This is abandonment in an emotive state. Frustration, anguish,
resignation: many of us have been there ourselves; the feeling that
things could not get any worse, that we have reached the bottom
of a metaphorical dark well and it is claustrophobic – there is no
way up and no one to pull us out. Desolation proves to be such an

all-consuming state that it is difficult to experience anything else that brings hope.

In a powerful reflection on Holy Week, Sheila Cassidy makes the point that taking this time seriously takes some walking through if we engage thoroughly with its cosmic relevance and grapple with its theological implications.[2] The desolation of Jesus is not to be imagined so much historically, she says: Christ's terrible scream emerges from the mother who has seen her children mutilated in front of her in a genocide the western world hears about only in retrospect. It is the exhaustion of an asylum seeker who ends up in a country with no money or friends to help him survive. Desolation lives daily.

Desolation is not only this deep desperation, it is also a sense of the loss of God, or a crushing sense of sin which is separating us from the divine loving embrace. At times, the medieval mystics experienced the sense that God was gone from them – or worse, that God did not really exist at all. Sometimes this stems from looking at the world in its overwhelming capacity for violence and evil, forgetting that the way God interacts with the world will always be mysterious and impossible for us to understand.

But perhaps this is not good enough. How often have we heard people express that they simply cannot believe in God when they look at the supposedly irredeemable state of the world? In the grip of desolation, many of the mystics and other theologians suggest the following:

> Only God fully knows the purpose of it. But the soul, which is humble enough to endure in faith, later glimpses what it is all about – but only later. The message at these points is to live through, groan, let yourself be broken open or be ignored by God. Above all, trust.[3]

The novel *The Shack* by the Canadian author William P. Young has become a worldwide phenomenon, perhaps because it presents a protagonist who grapples with this sense of desolation and the drain of faith that happens when it strikes. Young described the novel as 'a metaphor for the places you get stuck, you get hurt, you get damaged . . . the thing where shame or hurt is centred'.[4] The novel provides a creative and positive theological approach to the universal question of how to approach suffering and desolation.

The central character – a man known as Mack – does not know where to go with an all-consuming grief. While saving his son from drowning on a camping trip, Mack's daughter, Missy, was abducted and murdered by a serial killer. Her body and bloodied clothing have been discovered in an abandoned shack in the woods.

The book begins as Mack receives a letter inviting him to meet 'Papa' at the same shack. He takes courage and faces his worst nightmare of returning to that place of pain and grief. There he encounters personifications of the three persons of the Trinity, who welcome him warmly, soothing him through an offering of hospitality as well as absorbing some of his rawness. Most of the book narrates Mack's conversations with these three as he slowly moves from a place of utter desolation to one of new understanding, a new existential place, thanks to the gentleness of those who listen to and love him. Eventually he is led by Papa/the Father to the place where Missy's body was hidden. After his time at the cabin, Mack has a near-fatal car accident and, when he recovers, he becomes aware that his newly restored faith and subsequent healing has been worked through in what might be described as a 'holy dream'.

Although the novel inevitably had a mixed reception, it is arguably a brave attempt to describe the trajectory from an individual yet universal experience of desolation to one that moves into an emerging grace.

The wisdom Mack understands at the end of the novel is that the cross represents the astonishing reality that God's power never seeks to control. As Jesus is crucified, God's power stands silently while violence does its worst and rage is unleashed in all its fury. Love, however, does not intervene because it never seeks to control. Yet the cross illuminates a God who also resets the terms of such a conflict, moving the world ultimately through pain to new life, all catalysed through an absorption rather than a retaliation of violence, and culminating in an expansive love.

As we engage again with what must be the hardest moment in Holy Week, we remind ourselves that God was not and is never indifferent to the world's desolation, for he made the decisive choice to immerse himself in embodied form within the depths of humanity, born in a crib and dying on a cross. As people wrestling with faith, we make the choice: either God was not within Jesus and the cross becomes the ultimate symbol of a pointless existence because it takes us nowhere and will never redeem the powers of the world; or God was in Christ and the cross becomes the place where God understands all our desperation and loneliness, including death itself. And Christ is the one who has the final word on the world's suffering, through the love and new life that the resurrection promises.

Prejudice

The religious leaders are challenged by Jesus's authority
(Mark 11.27–33; 15.6–14, 16–19)

Prejudice is a burden that confuses the past, threatens the future and renders the present inaccessible.
(Maya Angelou, 1928–2014)[1]

In my early twenties, while exploring whether ordination was the path for me, I spent a year as a church intern in an ethnically diverse parish in West London. I made friends with several of the children of the Windrush generation and my limited, white world expanded. I heard stories of prejudice and of how it felt to struggle to simply gain the respect of the indigenous British population. I listened to the anger against ignorance, and was myself often the only white person at clandestine parties known as 'lock-ins', which happened at night-time in areas such as Harlesden and Willesden.

For the first time in my life, I learnt how it felt to be in a minority, which proved to be a profound and educative process. During that year, God's justice prerogative, which runs as rock strata through the biblical text, became my priority as my faith recalibrated its centre and expression. My parish priest had links with Christian radicals in Namibia, and while I had been at university Nelson Mandela had been released.

All of this began to superimpose on what had been an unconvincing and politically anaemic faith which was now transforming itself into a genuine thirst to play my own part in challenging injustice. I went to South Africa.

159

Prejudice will always be ingrained in the life of the world. The Old Testament is rife with warring tribes and long-standing feuds.

Jesus himself is often misunderstood: the jumped-up carpenter's son proclaiming he is God's chosen Messiah – not the expected military saviour the people are so desperate for. Those who are threatened by Jesus' natural prophetic persona demand to know on whose authority he is acting. But like most prophets, he bats the question back because they have missed the point.

The prophetic tradition raises people in every generation to illuminate the truth when it remains buried beneath a skewed and dysfunctional understanding of justice. Such people usually inhabit a big vision, one where there is a determined commitment to cross the road to the other side of experience, retaining a steadfast refusal to demonize 'the other'. Martin Luther King famously talked about an end to segregation because it was about the liberation of black *and* white people together.

Throughout his ministry, Jesus crosses those lines too. He ventures into Samaritan territory and encounters a woman at the well. Through his gentle acceptance of the offering that people bring, he connects all human need with God's compassionate heart. The sinful woman who washes his feet is no longer seen as the dregs of society but someone to be honoured because she has recognized the divine presence within Christ himself. At the end of his life, by his silence, Jesus refuses to allow the prejudice of others to label him as what he is not. But it happens anyway – he is vilified and ridiculed as 'The King of the Jews'. Great suffering follows as he is spat upon, humiliated, physically abused and finally killed. What happens to Jesus lives on in the atrocities that happen in Lebanon, Myanmar and on the Mexican–US border as people slip insidiously into racism rather than working to establish a non-conflictual and empathetic experience of a common humanity.

Spike Lee's recent production *BlacKkKlansman* (2018) is a film based on the true story of the infiltration and exposure of a local Ku Klux Klan collective in the 1970s. Set in Colorado Springs, the plot follows the rookie African-American detective Ron Stallworth and his Jewish colleague Flip Zimmerman.

The film has moments of 'black' comedy as the two police officers, working as a team, pretend to be new and interested white members as they draw both local as well as national KKK leaders into a scenario where the racism they are pretending to promote is exposed. They face great personal danger, but eventually the police operation is successful, and the team is congratulated by the Chief of Police, but this is in the aftermath of much extreme and ugly bigotry that is hard to watch. At one point a psychotic member of the local KKK group puts Zimmerman (who is Jewish) through a lie detector test at gunpoint. Using offensive language, he states that the Holocaust was a myth that simply did not happen.

Lee is a visionary director, his films exploring the interaction of an ethnically mixed community and the subtlety and complexity of how prejudice is discovered within it. For example, in *BlacKkKlansman*, Stallworth works hard to enable his colleague Zimmerman to get on board with the operation and, more importantly, to claim his Jewish identity for himself. As minorities, together they infiltrate the deeply evil Ku Klux Klan and shed light on its origins.

Prejudice brings so much pain for those on the receiving end, but it also diminishes those who hold indelible and unshifting bias. So much of this is about ignorance of who or what exists as 'the other'. It is also about the courage to build relationships with those whom we feel are alien (something we can all do, for we all meet those who are not from our race, class, faith, area and income bracket), and even if this is historic, it is about getting over long-standing suspicion and hatred. Fear of Muslims 'taking over' is often met with silence when the question is asked, 'Do you actually know anyone who is Muslim?'

Isaiah 2 contains the glorious vision of all peoples streaming to the Lord's holy mountain so that God might teach them his ways. Verse 4 says that he will be the ruler of all nations and will settle disputes for many people, that weapons of destruction will be transformed into tools to tend the earth. No longer will there be animosity between tribes.

As Christians, then, our charge is to be brave as Jesus was, to break down walls, to walk into the camp of the other, to find the common ground within our own humanity that can connect with another's, even though they might feel threatening to us or we might view them in anger as 'the enemy'.

In an extraordinary testimony to a life engaging with conflict and peacemaking, Peter Price tells many stories of engaging with this 'other' to break prejudices and build peace, suggesting that mostly this will be an uncomfortable experience for those brave enough to do it. He says:

> I am not a natural peacemaker. I enjoy a good fight. However, circumstances have frequently led me into situations where I have sensed an inner compulsion, a calling, to seek *the things that make for peace*. Those things are diverse, often disconnected, apparently insignificant, and their outcomes frequently questionable.[2]

There is something within the Christian vision that keeps us working at all of this, bravely as well as tentatively, through words and attitudes of kindness as well as challenge, whenever prejudice rears its head. We cross boundaries and break down walls to reach out in love to those who are vilified by the powerful, and who have suffered because of it.

Waiting

The women stand by the cross, waiting for Jesus to die
(John 19.25–27)

Three of the Gospels record Mary the mother of Jesus and various female companions waiting for Jesus to die (Matthew 27.55–56; Luke 23.49). The Fourth Gospel also includes the man whom theologians believe to be John, as Jesus entrusts Mary to this disciple's care. John's account describes this tiny group as being 'near the cross' while Luke and Matthew have the group set 'at a distance' or watching 'from a distance'.

What Mary and John do for Jesus becomes a universal statement of powerful love – they are with Jesus in solidarity until his earthly end. In a similar way, most of us would choose to journey until the end with a person whom we love a great deal, because love moves us beyond our own excruciating pain and keeps us faithful, with most of us choosing to 'be near'.

It is a hard, intense experience to wait for someone to die, especially someone we love. In 2003, my family and I rushed to visit my husband's 15-year-old nephew in hospital. He had been diagnosed with a brain tumour. Our own son was just months old and we took him to the hospital, where Adam was able to hold him briefly. In the hospital café, my sister-in-law told us that she would not leave the hospital until her son had died. It was an intense, agonizing wait for us all, particularly for her and my brother-in-law. Such times we never forget.

Waiting commences and ends Jesus' life. As it begins, Simeon and Anna wait in the temple to see the Lord, their own deaths dependent on glimpsing the chosen Messiah. Anna, we are told, has been continually in the temple, fasting and praying. For both of these elderly people there is an energy and an expectation set amid the wait. Finally, the contemplative yet exuberant words of the Nunc Dimittis are uttered by Simeon as he praises God, understanding that he can finally die in spiritual peace (Luke 2.29–32). Now, at the end and near to the cross, Jesus' friends and family wait for the end of this extraordinary life.

These days we are not good at waiting. In the supermarket queue we get impatient when the checkout assistant spends too long talking to the person in front of us. Every minute of our time feels so precious, so vital, with the sense that we should not waste any minute of it. In an era when so many experiences are instantaneous with rapid communication and travel, our tolerance for waiting for anything has diminished. Yet waiting is both positive and negative. In the Christian tradition it is associated with darkness as well as with light, and with the slow revelation of the wisdom of God, which is what the prophet Job and so many of the sentiments in the Psalms grapple with.

The French theologian Jacques Ellul offers some profound thoughts on the darkness of waiting: 'The person of hope is the person who waits, and with a pessimistic waiting, for *normally* nothing should happen.' Job, he says, is enveloped within the silence of God, and as he waits, he is derided by others, is proved wrong, loses faith in God's power to break into his life, but still he waits.

> Just as Job is the one who attests that a person serves God for nothing, he is also the one in whom the fullness of waiting is actualized. He never lets himself be diverted to the right or to the left by his own attempts to transform the situation . . . He rejects all those human reactions because he knows that the root of the problem is not there. He leaves activity and work to one side, since the one important thing is the wait for God.[1]

Waiting amid pain and suffering is essentially biblical, but with it comes a potent injection of a hope and a yearning for God to rescue and redeem. Waiting requires us to be hopeful, and it gives us space to be so. Potentially, waiting strengthens us because it encourages us to live well and fully in the present, often providing us with time to think things through and to find a solution or what might be the way forward for our lives. But waiting can also be a part of darkness as we wait for harder things, such as the results of medical tests or for justice to be done. Enforced waiting means we feel out of control; it is a place where anger and resentment rise.

On 14 June 2017, 72 people were killed in Grenfell Tower, a 24-storey block of flats that caught fire in North Kensington, West London. Another 256 were made homeless. It was the deadliest residential fire in the UK since the Second World War. The incident shocked the nation, who could not quite believe that such a tragedy could happen in a developed and sophisticated western country. Inevitably, the government promised swift rehousing, but the scale of this proved to be far more complex than was initially understood. The promised few weeks of staying in temporary hotel accommodation turned into months for many residents, and even in 2019 many were still waiting to be rehoused. Resentment has built as legalities surrounding the use of materials, whose safety had not been comprehensively tested and regulated, have not been owned by the local council, despite residents' groups highlighting concerns over fire regulations years earlier.

The incident has been characterized by waiting – for accommodation, for accurate information and for local and national accountability. The charred shell of Grenfell has become a symbol of the pain of waiting, of procrastination, of the frustration of dealing with a complex situation, of the inevitable reality that it is the poorest and most marginalized who so often have the longest wait for genuine justice.

In Holy Week, it is Holy Saturday that we associate most with waiting, with overtones of relief and resignation as well as a strange expectancy. We wait and we watch within the vigil many churches offer as the Easter candle is processed into a darkened church, symbolic of the dawn joy of the resurrection. Two thousand years on, we know and believe that Jesus lives again, that God is not dead. We are the privileged ones. But for those who wait but do not know the outcome, the capacity for miracle and for hope feels much harder. As W. H. Vanstone says, 'Waiting can be the most intense and poignant of all human experiences – the experience which, above all others, strips us of our needs, our values and ourselves.'[2]

Prayer and action

- How has your own experience of painful situations shaped your life and changed and/or developed your faith?
- How can we help those who are hurting, both in our own churches and further afield? Has God given you a heart for an individual, a group or a community that is suffering? Create a prayer list and commit to praying each day for someone who is in pain.
- Compare and contrast Jesus' leadership with Pilate's. Did both cause pain as well as satisfaction?
- When have you felt dislocated from a situation or community, out of place and out of sorts somewhere? Who might be feeling this in our own church, school or community? What can we do as a community of faith to alleviate the pain of those who feel like this? Pray for those who continuously feel that they don't fit in.
- Have you had experiences of desolation in your life? If so, how have you come through these, or how has God enabled you to come through them? How could you help someone who feels like this? Pray for organizations that listen and support those who feel at their lowest, such as the Samaritans.
- Have you been on the receiving end of prejudice in your life? How did you, or do you, challenge it when it happens or when you hear it spoken randomly? How does prejudice manifest itself within your church and/or community? Pray for all those who suffer because of unprecedented ignorance.
- When have you had to wait for something significant in your life or accompanied someone else through a time of waiting? Reflect

on this experience. Where was God within it? Often, waiting with someone else is a great gift to them and means they do not have to undertake the journey on their own. Could you offer this ministry to someone you know, even in a small way?

AFTER EASTER

Miracle

Mary Magdalene and Simon Peter discover that Jesus has been raised from the dead (John 20.1–10)

A miracle in the sense of the New Testament is not so much a breach of the laws of nature, but rather a remarkable or exceptional occurrence which brought an undeniable sense of the presence and power of God .
(Charles Harold Dodd, 1884–1973)[1]

Out of the gloom of a cold dawn emerges the most astonishing event. The dead Christ does not lie in the unsettling peace of the tomb. A mystery pervades the garden, for Jesus was dead when he was taken down from the cross. We know the rest of the story, and it is miraculous: this is the point when faith must make the decisive leap from rational explanation into the territory of belief in bodily resurrection. Such new perception brings hope and the understanding that all life is held within divine grace. The resurrection tells us that the life of God can never be constrained or killed, and that God has ultimate power over death. Such life is the glorious gift that is open to all people.

Miracles truly happen. There are what might be described as 'God-incidences' – events and circumstances that contravene the natural laws of the universe: sick people get better; people or opportunities emerge at exactly the right time, often against the odds. The Gospels are miracle-abundant, and we diminish these if we explain them away as metaphors alone. Yet there is also a sense that within all life there resides a divine dynamic, one that lies at the heart of the Easter story – an energy of cyclical birth and death and then new life.

The power of miracle is a theme that runs through all the chapters in this book, miracle being an element that transforms a wilderness state of existence to one filled with a sudden grace which opens the future. In terms of *appetite*, Jesus multiplies food to feed a hungry crowd in the feeding of the five thousand, and he produces fine wine for wedding guests to feast upon at Cana (John 6.1–13; 2.1–10).

Through miracle, Jesus often restores *identity*. In healing the man known as the Gerasene Demoniac, Jesus restores his dignity, identity and composure as he transfers the harmful forces from this tormented soul into a herd of pigs (Luke 8.26–39). Many of the healing miracles have Jesus challenging assumptions of what is thought to be unclean. This man has named himself 'Mob', or 'Legion', indicating that his individual identity has been overtaken by, possessed by, a whole regiment of demons. As Jesus repeats the command for these to 'come out' three times, he makes a connection that this false identity is associated with death and impurity. Through his actions, Jesus makes a statement that nothing masters any person's identity except the God of life who liberates all from that which enslaves them. The adversary bows low, recognizing the identity of Jesus himself, Son of the Most High God, who forces him to reveal his name. Mob's true identity is reclaimed from all that creates false personhood, and it is achieved through an encounter with Christ himself.

In the Bible, Jesus restores professional reputation as well as morale as he tells his fishermen disciples to cast the net on the other side as they float towards the shore after a depressing night catching nothing (John 21.3–6). Through that miracle he connects and honours their earthly *occupation* because he understands that it is their livelihood and vital for their survival. But through it he also makes new connections with the vision he has for the world and cleverly invites them to participate in it. He makes links between the job of fishermen and a life lived in Christ, and he does it through a miracle.

The incredible story of the healing of a paralyzed man, whose friends take off some of the roof to place him in front of Jesus, speaks of the new *freedom* given to many people Christ heals, as the man literally gets up and walks out of the room (Luke 5.17–26). The miracles Jesus undertakes set people free to live in the Spirit, their lives lived to the full once more: he restores sight to the blind man and heals the lepers of a disease that socially as well as physically stigmatizes them. Jesus performs miracles often because of two key elements: a person's faith and his own heart of compassion, because he yearns to alleviate another's pain. There is nothing more tragic than the death of a young person. The raising of Jairus' daughter (Luke 8.40–56) feels particularly poignant because our children are bound to us through a depth of love we often find difficult to articulate. In this story, a whole crowd is in mourning, and Jesus restores a new joy for a community as well as for an individual family.

Jesus demonstrates that he is Lord over the forces of nature when he calms the storm (Luke 8.22–25). The disciples, despite their knowledge of being out on the water, are in a state of high *anxiety* as a squall blows up unpredictably. Jesus wakes, gets up and commands the winds to cease. 'Where is your faith?' he asks them. This story is a metaphor for all the tumult not only outside us but within us too as he enfolds his friends with his peace.

One of the most touching and moving miracles in the Gospels is the raising of Lazarus (John 11), perhaps because Jesus has a personal connection with this small family of Martha, Mary and their brother, but it is significant too because of the choice he makes by doing it. By performing such a public miracle, Jesus highlights his reputation as radical prophet yet again, someone who threatens the authority of the religious groups of the time who are already gunning for his demise.

This is the last time Jesus uses his God-given powers before beginning his journey to the cross. His tears of grief are a recognition of his anguish. After this, a panicked Caiaphas calls together the Sanhedrin, the leaders of the Jews, to authorize the elimination of Jesus. Lazarus' life is effectively exchanged for the offering of his own death. Miracle here is sacrificial as well as life-giving. Jesus' *pain* is ambiguous – his tears are joyful because of the happiness he has given back to Martha and Mary, but they signify the realization of the terrible reality of his own passion which is to come.

Jean Vanier says this:

> This text of Lazarus brings each of us back to the tomb within, where anguish dwells. Jesus does not want to set us free. He will not always take away our insecurities, but he will give us a new force to accept them, to become conscious of them, and to live with them: 'I will put my Spirit in you.' Jesus wants to put his Spirit in us, so that we will no longer be men and women driven by fear, but free people, free to love.[2]

The miracle of the resurrection is the miracle of this new possibility for a grace-filled eternity.

Hope

The Emmaus Road
(Luke 24.13–35)

The Christian hope – a combination of progressive faith and responsive love – is, in the end, what makes our pilgrimage possible at all.

(Gerald Priestland, 1927–91)[1]

Two narratives of hope have recently caught my attention.

The first, *Believer*, is a BBC documentary featuring Dan Reynolds, the lead singer of the US indie band Imagine Dragons.[2] Reynolds is an unashamed Mormon and has become increasingly disturbed by the rising suicide rate among gay and bisexual young people in his home state of Utah. In 2007, 60.7 per cent of the population considered themselves members of The Church of Jesus Christ of Latter-Day Saints (LDS), although a smaller number considered themselves to be practising members.

Like many conservative religious groups, Mormonism does not support the practice of homosexuality, and often publicly condemns it as a sin. Over the last few years, Reynolds has used his rock-star status to hold an annual concert – LoveLoud – to try to challenge this firmly held belief and to highlight its tragic consequences.

Reynolds himself is not gay but is married with a growing 'traditional' family, and this moving documentary charts his gentle but persuasive diplomacy in a message to the most powerful within the Mormon Church, his unstinting loyalty to it and his compassion for those who have lost sons and daughters to suicide.

As Christians, we do not go along with Mormonism's doctrinal beliefs, but there seem to be plenty of kingdom values in Reynolds' crusade. His attitude clearly states that people need the Church, that it is essentially part of a culture that creates a powerful sense of belonging, of providing sound and wise values to live a fruitful life of joy and service. And yet there are ambiguous and destructive elements that need to change, for they lead others to loathe themselves and to believe that they cannot live tenably in the world of their birthright.

The prophets of our age emerge so often from the popular music arena, and this is who the younger generation often listen to. Imagine Dragons, my son's favourite band, is creating a brave new world, it seems.

The second narrative comes from the *Church Times*, in an issue devoted to climate change.[3] Within its pages was an array of articles dedicated to the many different aspects of a challenging problem that affects the whole of the planet, to varying degrees. While there was a fair dose of factual reality, there was also plenty of hope. One article was entitled 'Cheer Up: Climate Change Can Be Stopped', which described the serious commitment of several countries to reducing or phasing out fossil fuels completely and replacing them with renewable energy sources. Another article focused on how Germany, with the demise of the coal industry, is putting serious measures in place to provide its workers with opportunities for retraining. Joe Ware, a journalist and writer for Christian Aid, suggested to readers five steps by which they could begin to make a difference – always a challenge when Christians feel potentially overwhelmed by the scale of a global problem.

It was interesting to note my own response to this comprehensive read. I admit that climate change is something I feel passionate about, but on reading all this I felt there were now more things I personally could begin to do to play my part. Roughly speaking, these could be put into the categories of changes of behaviour and habits, linking with others and communication.

In the astonishing story in Luke 24, we experience something of the dynamics many of us feel when we are faced with the enormity of a problem like climate change. It is easy to feel despondent, and this is certainly how the disciples are feeling as they trudge out of Jerusalem towards the small village of Emmaus. They are carrying the huge loss of Jesus' inspiring vision as well as of his physical presence with them. Initially, they do not recognize Jesus.

Sometimes, when we feel overwhelmed with anxiety or by the size of a problem, we are unable see where the solution might lie and are temporarily blinded by depression, as the disciples are. But it is through communication that eyes begin to open and spirits are restored. This stranger takes them back to the foretelling from the prophets and Moses, and to promises of hope; he somehow makes them feel better, more enabled and empowered to face the future. As Jesus breaks bread with them, they suddenly understand that they have been walking in the presence of the same Lord they have been mourning and admit that their hearts have been stirred through the encounter with him. Their hopeful solution lies within their present existence, which sets out a future pathway too.

The two disciples are possessed with new fire; they find the other disciples and excitedly tell of their own hope and belief that Jesus is indeed alive, for he has come among them. The following verses describe this happening again, as Jesus leaves them with a sense of residing peace.

Hope often arises in times of great depression and despondency. True hope cannot be implemented without the energy of Christ, which many people are pulled and pushed by even if they cannot name the power of Jesus within it. In this incident the disciples are restored by hope, after they have experienced as well as recognized Christ in their lives. This fact alone re-energizes them to follow through with the vision he shared and advocated during his earthly life.

Hope, therefore, has to be active. It does not sit as an attractive proposition, a show home that is admired but which no one really inhabits. Hope means participation in some shape or form, or it means an active change of heart, of attitude, of perspective or of lifestyle. Hope can awaken new meaning in a life of hidden desperation, which so many live with to some degree or other.

Hope resides too in the middle ground between institution and prophetic edge, between that which is known and believed and that which is yet to come to fruition. The wilderness of human experience in a western context means we so often fall into a deep cynicism, believing that hope is somehow naïve, as outside forces flatten all our attempts to live by it.

The Brazilian philosopher Rubem A. Alves likened life to a dance. He said that living is like dancing, and as someone dances, they move their body according to the rhythm and harmony which fills the space. He says:

> You may dance the tune played by the present reality. Your style of life will be realistic and pragmatic. Or you may choose to move your body under the spell of a mysterious tune and rhythm which comes from a world we do not see, the world of our hopes and aspirations. Hope is hearing the melody of the future. Faith is to dance it. You risk your life, and you take your risk to its ultimate conclusion, even the cross.[4]

Joy

Jesus is taken up to heaven
(Luke 24.50–53)

Joy is the infallible sign of the presence of God.
(Teilhard de Chardin, 1881–1955)[1]

This week one of my children has experienced a crushing disappointment, and as a parent I feel it intensely. Through it, I have absorbed many things – anger, frustration – and I have railed at the injustice in life. The happiness I was expecting to feel on behalf of my child has been absent.

It proves a hard discipline to believe in joy's power when we are feeling far from it. Genuine joy is quite a long way from these shores because it provides a deeper platform of faith stability, where we can rest in the knowledge that our lives are mysteriously held in the love and plans that God has for us and the world. We may not know quite what we mean when we quote Julian of Norwich's famous mantra that 'All things will be well', but it feels strangely comforting as well as true.

This kind of joy pushes through disappointment, bereavement and misery. It is robust, with the ability to infiltrate and lift the heaviness of sadness. It is no small coincidence that joy is the quality that provides the overarching finale to all the Gospels. Grief and anxiety intermingle in the certainty that Jesus will make no further ghostly appearances after the Emmaus Road experience hits home. The disciples understand that theirs is to be a joy-filled inheritance and promotion of the kingdom vision, not without cost or suffering, but one that must have joy as its overarching characteristic.

The presence of God through the fellowship of the Spirit will sustain this and accompany them, a power to be drawn on in a brand-new way. To mark this, Jesus takes them out of the city, blesses them and departs to heaven. The disciples are overcome, after so much confusion and trauma, with great joy, and they are inspired to go to their traditional place of worship, the temple, to thank and praise God.

We can live out this idea of blessing as followers of Jesus. Even at the end of a bad day we thank God for those people who bring blessing into our lives, those whose presence inspires us to be grounded and grateful. Life is rarely all contentment or all pain; it is usually a good mixture of both, which intertwine in the complexity of life. In Jesus, Friedrich von Hügel says, we discover a strong and ultimate personality who teaches us the true attitude to suffering:

With him . . . there is the union of the clearest, keenest sense of all the mysterious depth and breadth and length and height of human sadness, suffering and sin, *and*, in spite of this and through this and at the end of this, a note of conquest and of triumphant joy.[2]

We have a choice, as followers of Jesus, to inhabit joy and to believe in its hopeful power to reconfigure our attitude and approach to the setbacks we experience as well as the general attitude we take to our lives. This provides a witness to others who are mystified by the unfairness and immense suffering which can drench any of us like a freezing and unexpected shower. Henri Nouwen says that joy does not simply happen to us. We must choose joy and keep choosing it every day.

The film *Mamma Mia 2* has this in bucketloads. I would surmise that many went to see this riotous and high-spirited film to inject a bit of joy into what can often feel like a hard life. But even if life does not feel like this, joy is good for us; it feels beneficial to immerse ourselves in this, to know that life can be colourful and funny, that it can renew our energy to bring us genuine delight. The film is the follow-up to the 2008 hit musical and uses the exuberant music of

ABBA to provide a joy-infused cocktail in the midst of difficult life circumstances and new beginnings. It is both a prequel as well as a sequel, taking us back to Donna Sheridan's arrival on the Greek island of Kalokairi in the late 1970s, where she became pregnant and gave birth to her treasured daughter Sophie, alone and penniless. The film also charts Sophie's own return to the island as she attempts to begin a hotel business, which is subsequently ruined by a terrible storm on the eve of the reopening of the hotel.

Sophie is pregnant herself and emotionally embroiled in a problematic and long-distance relationship, so she has these things to deal with as well. In real life, these kinds of events would often be difficult to resolve and would not generate an immediately positive response. The inimitable music from ABBA, as music so often does, lifts the challenging gloom to present an alternative future, one in which hard things do not *not* happen but where joy makes it possible for us to live through them in faith and hope – genuinely. Laughter, sunshine, companionship, the recalibration of attitude and the promise of a future spur this on joy's way.

Joy, therefore, is not an absence of wilderness necessarily, neither is it a carefree life. Joy resides in the blessings of the present moment as well as in the potential of a future filled with the significance of a resurrected life.

C. S. Lewis's famous partial autobiography, *Surprised by Joy*, is an exemplification of this idea. Published in 1955, the book describes the author's conversion to Christianity, which had taken place 24 years earlier. But Lewis's main aim was to identify and describe the events surrounding his accidental discovery of and subsequent longing for the phenomenon he called 'joy'. He was struck by moments or 'stabs' of joy throughout his life. Perhaps this is an accurate description of how these waves also overcome us at times, often mystically. Lewis's journey was one that moved from atheism to theism, from theism to Christian faith, and he described joy as a signpost to himself and others who feel lost, who live a life where joy has simply left the building. The book alludes to Wordsworth's famous poem of the same title, 'Surprised by Joy – Impatient as the Wind' (1815), which relates to a single moment when the poet forgot the death of his daughter, temporarily relinquishing his grief.

Just after midnight on New Year's Eve, when I look outside at the black sky, there are hundreds of diaphanous Chinese lanterns which have been launched into the cold night. Glowing orange, they seem a particularly poignant symbol of a joyous hope, ascending into the sky, heralding an insistent statement that the coming year will be a positive one, setting aside the problems of the past 12 months and trusting that such joy will carry us through. This is not the absence of sorrow or darkness but a reminder that kindness, deep peace, trust and hope are all manifestations of a joy that slowly builds robust spiritual strength, steadfast friendship, a sense of perspective, gratitude and the ability to transform a cup that feels half empty to one that is actually half full.

Grace

A life lived in God is a life lived in grace
(John 1.14; James 4.6)

Each moment of our existence, we are either growing into more or retreating into less.
(Brennan Manning, 1934–2013)[1]

In 2018, the grime artist and rapper Stormzy produced the powerful song 'Blinded by Your Grace'. The song describes beautifully the experience of the artist being blown away by the power of God's grace in a life that has been lived in the shadows. Its lyrics describe the naming of brokenness, of being unworthy, but also include recognition that the grace of God lifts us up to a better place, saving us from the narcissism of ourselves. Although Stormzy has never openly talked about his faith, Christian spirituality comes through loud and clear in the lyrics and titles of his songs and albums. In this song, the experience of grace is so meaningful that it is as though he has been overcome, literally 'blinded'.

Stormzy got to number one in the charts with this song and has gained massive popularity in mainstream UK culture as well as with the younger generation in the Church. Rap music emerges from positive and negative life experiences, and it is refreshing that a song like this can communicate an authentic experience of what existential, grace-filled faith feels like.

The mystical first chapter of John's Gospel describes the Word coming into the world as a human being. Two essential qualities of this person are truth and grace, which are *lived among us*. Thus, these have to be lived and experienced.

Grace is a dangerous word, a quality that easily becomes a religious platitude, something conceptual we know we ought to embrace but sometimes struggle to feel and truly inhabit. This is because we are shaped by our own and others' value systems, which so often bring a 'justification by works' consciousness.

A few years ago, in the church where I was, we began a food bank. It made the headlines because it happened to be in the then Chancellor of the Exchequer's own constituency, a wealthy area of the country. The parish nevertheless embraced the project, and several years on there is still a steady stream of people who need the service. But there were also rumblings and grumblings of discontent among the volunteers, who would often pass judgement on those who came. Eyebrows would be raised when a client arrived in a car or with a dog, or smelling of cigarettes, as though poverty should look and behave in a specific way that is 'deserving'. But such attitudes are understandable, and we should not judge, for they arise from lives where financial security and a certain standard of living have been hard work and sometimes hard won.

It's perhaps only natural to understand a situation from our own life experience. But food banks also offer other gifts of grace: some kindness and companionship in an otherwise lonely day, a gift that someone does not have to compete or fight for, vital supplies with no strings attached, an open door and warm space just for a while – a contrast to a stressful queue or a cold and lonely flat. Here is grace.

Figen Murray's son Martyn was killed in the bomb that exploded in Manchester on 22 May 2017 when Ariana Grande was performing. Martyn had been due to leave to go travelling in the US the following day, an adventure he had been planning for two years. The devastation to his family's emotional and spiritual well-being has inevitably been terrible, but Figen has chosen to respond to the event with extraordinary understanding and forgiveness. She says:

I can honestly say that I feel no resentment towards Salman Abedi. In that moment, he believed that he was doing the right thing. That's why I've made the conscious choice to forgive him – hate only breeds hate. Now more than ever, this world needs humanity and kindness.[2]

She makes the illuminating point that out of a deeply bad situation, ironically, goodness has arisen. The boy who detonated the bomb achieved the opposite of what he wanted – he caused an explosion of love, as family, friends and strangers came together in solidarity and courage. Figen's daughter Nikita took one of her GCSEs on the anniversary of Martyn's death, determined to sit the exam. She eventually achieved 11 A* grades. Here, too, is unimaginable grace.

This book concludes by asking its readers to be challenged to live from a position of conscious grace rather than from a place of expectation, judgement or victimhood. My own journey over the last few years has brought me to a place of deep humility, knowing that I am far more likely to experience God's gifts when I set my own expectations lower than they have been previously in all areas of my life. We are far more likely to live our lives seeing and understanding the action and energy of God when we do this, for here is also the place from where the poorest, meekest and most broken automatically live their lives. When we lower our expectations, we are more likely to finish each day with gratitude rather than dissatisfaction, identifying where and how God has filled that day with his grace, even amid the ache of wilderness.

Those closest to understanding what grace means are people who have a profound sense of their own undeservedness, those who know that this grace is an immense, almost burdensome gift that they are learning to accept, and are learning to see others and themselves as loved and loveable, however imperfect or unworthy they might be. But when such an understanding is really grasped, it feels startling, and it is transformative as we begin to live life with a cup that is half full rather than one that feels half empty.

The BBC One series *Broken*, starring Sean Bean as Catholic priest Michael Kerrigan, encapsulates what a grace-filled life and ministry might look like. The series presents a variety of individuals who seek out Fr Michael's counsel and compassion as they lay before him their ragged and complex lives within the close-knit northern town where they live. Thorny 'wilderness' problems of the poverty trap, the desperation of deep debt, sexuality and how to remain honourable in an institution are all dealt with by this very human priest from a place of exquisite grace which is offered into realistic situations that do not have the luxury of being easily resolved.

Michael's life is bleak and lonely; he is caring for his mother, who is a train ride away, and his relentless ministry seems devoid of easy resolutions to the eternal pastoral problems that come his way. He lives wilderness daily, mostly by absorbing other people's pain and anger, just as Jesus so often did. Towards the end of the series he falls into an understandable despondency and we sense that he is on the edge of resignation and walking away from his life, the Church and perhaps even God. But as he celebrates the Mass one day, while distributing the Sacrament he is swept up into a renewed sense of grace as, astounded, he watches all those he has tried (and perhaps failed) to help process up to the altar. As they hold out their hands for broken bread, we hear the whisper from each of them, 'You are a good priest.' It is an immensely moving piece of television and one where the essence of faith and the wonder of grace is successfully interpreted.

All the concepts in this book are ones where both wilderness and grace reside together, which is so often the nature of life itself. Wilderness is soothed by kindness; an unexpected gift; an invitation; a challenge; an acceptance; an offer of help; a perspective of hope; a belief that this is not the final state, situation or the final word; and through the recognition that the world is still beautiful. Christ communicated what God's grace looked like, and we too need to recognize the signs each day. As Gerard Manley Hopkins famously said, 'The world is charged with the grandeur of God.'[3]

The sacred is infused, embedded and intertwined in a grace-filled as well as hard-bitten world. Living by and with and through grace means that we see this, we name it and we experience this gift, whether we are so-called people of faith or simply on a journey to faith of some kind. In the words of a holy friend, 'Our ordinary places are already alive with an extraordinary God.' Sometimes we sense this vaguely, mysteriously in the air, while at other times we are overcome as grace lasers into our life, overwhelming us with transformation.

As Christ's followers, we choose how we respond to what happens to us in our lives, but we will see more and understand more of who God is if we live as gracious and grace-filled people even when trudging through the darkness. People notice and are affected, sometimes even changed, through encounters with those who understand the power of grace in their lives. As the quote at the beginning of the chapter suggests, grace grows larger and hearts become more loving, enabling us to be more expansive people. We aspire to be such people, for they are stained with love.

Notes

Introduction
1 Rowan Williams, *Being Disciples* (London: SPCK, 2016), pp. 3, 6.

Week 1
Introduction: appetite
1 By kind permission of friend and poet Jan Dean.
2 Tobias Jones, *A Place of Refuge* (London: Quercus Books, 2015), pp. 184–5.
3 Jones, *A Place of Refuge*, pp. 184–5.

Hunger
1 Michel Quoist, cited in Hannah Ward and Jennifer Wild (comp.), *The Lion Christian Quotation Collection* (Oxford: Lion, 1997), p. 298.
2 'Madagascar's starving "are surviving on locusts"', *Church Times*, 6 January 2017, <https://www.churchtimes.co.uk/articles/2017/6-january/news/world/madagascar-s-starving-are-surviving-on-locusts>.
3 FAO, IFAD, UNICEF, WFP and WHO, 'The State of Food Security and Nutrition in the World 2017', 2017, <https://docs.wfp.org/api/documents/WFP-0000022419/download/?_ga=2.3057968.1862024812.1563552653-437857931.1563552653>.
4 Oxford English Dictionary, <https://www.lexico.com/en/definition/hunger>.
5 Tim Wyatt, 'Scottish MP takes on week of oats, beans and rice to highlight African subsistence-level diets', *Church Times*, 31 March 2017, <https://www.churchtimes.co.uk/articles/2017/31-march/news/uk/scottish-mp-takes-on-week-of-oats-beans-and-rice-to-highlight-african-subsistence-level-diets>.
6 Ronald Sider, *Rich Christians in an Age of Hunger* (London: Hodder and Stoughton, 1978), p. 120.

Fast

1 Attributed to Mike Bickle. Source unknown.
2 *Lose Weight for Good*, BBC, January 2018.
3 Martin Thornton, *A Joyful Heart* (London: SPCK, 1987), p. 10.

Feast

1 Susan Wiggs, *The Apple Orchard* (Don Mills, Ontario: MIRA Books, 2013), p. 138.
2 Terence Handley MacMath, 'Interview: Bill Sewell, restaurateur', *Church Times*, 24 March 2017, <https://www.churchtimes.co.uk/articles/2017/24-march/features/interviews/interview-bill-sewell-restaurateur>.

Excess

1 Carole Cadwalladr, 'The Real Junk Food Project: Revolutionising how we tackle food waste', *The Guardian*, 18 September 2016, <https://www.theguardian.com/lifeandstyle/2016/sep/18/real-junk-food-project-revolutionising-how-we-tackle-food-waste>.

Bread for the world

1 Ryan Cook, 'Things I've Learned from 2.5 Years of Opening Our Home on Monday Evenings', Metagnosis blog, 14 February 2018, <https://metagnosis.xyz/things-ive-learned-from-2-5-years-of-opening-our-home-on-monday-evenings/>. All extracts used with permission.
2 Cook, 'Things I've Learned'.
3 Cook, 'Things I've Learned'.

Week 2

Introduction: identity

1 My own poem.
2 Rowan Williams, *Being Human* (London: SPCK, 2018), pp. 58–60.

Name

1 Mindy Weisberger, 'Say Goodbye to the World's Oldest Spider, Dead at 43', LiveScience, 1 May 2018, <https://www.livescience.com/62452-worlds-oldest-spider-dies.html>.

Loneliness

1 Gail Honeyman, *Eleanor Oliphant Is Completely Fine* (London: HarperCollins, 2017), epigraph.
2 Marcus Borg, *Days of Awe and Wonder* (London: SPCK, 2017), p. 199.
3 Borg, *Days of Awe and Wonder*, p. 200.

Solitude

1 Kate Kellaway, 'Sara Maitland: "My subconscious was cleverer than my conscious in choosing to live alone"', *The Guardian*, 2 February 2014, <https://www.theguardian.com/theobserver/2014/feb/02/sara-maitland-how-to-be-alone-interview>.
2 Abbot Moses, cited in Hannah Ward and Jennifer Wild (comp.), *The Lion Christian Quotation Collection* (Oxford: Lion, 1997), p. 30.
3 Verena Schiller, *A Simplified Life* (Norwich: Canterbury Press, 2010).
4 Kellaway, 'Sara Maitland'.

Friendship

1 Jürgen Moltmann, *The Open Church* (London: SCM Press, 1978), p. 51.
2 James Nelson, *The Intimate Connection* (London: SPCK, 1992), p. 65.
3 Thanks to the Revd Graham Green for this story.
4 Nell Goddard, 'I'll Be There for You? Connecting with Culture', LICC, 4 January 2018, <https://www.licc.org.uk/resources/thereforyou/>.

Community

1 Jean Vanier, *Community and Growth* (London: Darton, Longman and Todd, 2006), p. 56.
2 Vanier, *Community and Growth*, p. 56.
3 Vanier, *Community and Growth*, p. 56.

Week 3
Introduction: occupation

1 My own poem.
2 Raymond B. Blakney (trans.), 'The Treatises', Chapter 72, in *Meister Eckhart: A Modern Translation* (New York: Harper Torchbooks, 1941), pp. 10–11.

3 François de la Fénelon, *Selections from the Writings of Fénelon*, trans. 'Mrs Follen' (Edward T. Whitfield, 1850), p. 246.

Ambition

1 Tim Winton, *Cloudstreet* (New York: Picador, 1991).
2 Anthony Ashley Cooper, Earl of Shaftesbury (1801–85), cited in Hannah Ward and Jennifer Wild (comp.), *The Lion Christian Quotation Collection* (Oxford: Lion, 1997), p. 190.
3 Marianne Williamson, *A Return to Love* (London: HarperCollins, 1996), chapter 7, 'Work'.
4 Paul Bradbury, 'A Vocational Journey', *Guidelines September–December 2018: Bible study for today's ministry and mission*, July 2017, pp. 7–10.
5 William Shakespeare, *Julius Caesar*, Act 3, Scene 1.
6 Shakespeare, *Julius Caesar*, Act 3, Scene 2.
7 William Shakespeare, *Henry VIII*, Act 3, Scene 2.
8 Edmund Burke, cited in Ward and Wild, *The Lion Christian Quotation Collection*, p. 142.

Position

1 Barbara Brown Taylor, *An Altar in the World: Finding the sacred beneath our feet* (Norwich: Canterbury Press, 2009), pp. 138–9.
2 This is a slightly edited version of Lamdin's story. Keith Lamdin, *Finding Your Leadership Style* (London: SPCK, 2012), chapter 1.
3 Thomas Merton, cited on Goodreads (italics added), <https://www.goodreads.com/quotes/38593-do-not-depend-on-the-hope-of-results-you-may>.

Contribution

1 Mother Teresa, cited in Shane Claiborne, *The Irresistible Revolution* (Grand Rapids, MI: Zondervan, 2006), p. 319.

Vocation

1 Metropolitan Anthony Bloom, cited in Hannah Ward and Jennifer Wild (comp.), *The Lion Christian Quotation Collection* (Oxford: Lion, 1997), p. 233.

2 I am indebted to the Revd Ann Turner for her permission to publish this story, which she often tells at the end of Bishops' Advisory Panels.

Service

1 Basilea Schlink, cited in Hannah Ward and Jennifer Wild (comp.), *The Lion Christian Quotation Collection* (Oxford: Lion, 1997), p. 307.
2 Ghislaine Howard is a well-known artist working in the north west of England.
3 Jean Vanier, *The Gospel of John, The Gospel of Relationship* (London, Darton, Longman and Todd, 2016), p. 90.

Week 4
Introduction: freedom

1 My own poem.
2 Ananias Mpunzi, 'Black Theology as Liberation Theology', in *Black Theology: The South African voice*, ed. Basil Moore (London: C. Hurst & Co, 1973), p. 133.

Boundary

1 Muthuraj Swamy, *Reconciliation* (London: SPCK, 2019), p. 4.
2 Roberto Bolaño, cited in *Celtic Daily Prayer Book Two* (London: Longman, Green and Co., 1949), p. 1422.
3 Swamy, *Reconciliation*, p. 7.
4 'Representative Gonzalez on the Government Shutdown and Border Security', C-Span, 16 January 2019, <https://www.c-span. org/video/?456994-4/washington-journal-representative-vicente-gonzalez-d-texas-discusses-government-shutdown-border>.
5 Walter Brueggemann, cited in Hannah Ward and Jennifer Wild (comp.), *The Lion Christian Quotation Collection* (Oxford: Lion, 1997), p. 238.

Safety

1 Johann Wolfgang von Goethe, cited at <https://quotefancy.com/ quote/839584/Johann-Wolfgang-von-Goethe>.

2 Michelle Obama, *Becoming* (New York: Viking Press, 2018), p. 75.

3 'Mohsin Hamid on leaving home', BBC Radio 4, *Start the Week*, 29 January 2018, presented by Kirsty Wark and discussing migration and expanding borders with Mohsin Hamid, lawyer Carol Bohmer, theatre director Robert Hastie and former Portuguese minister Bruno Maçães, <https://www.bbc.co.uk/programmes/b09pjgdg>.

4 *Crossing Birmingham's Invisible Borders*, BBC One, 2 February 2018.

Denial

1 Jim Butcher, *Cold Days* (New York: New American Library, 2013).

2 Brennan Manning, *The Ragamuffin Gospel* (Colorado Springs, CO: Multnomah Books, 1990), p. 135.

3 Manning, *The Ragamuffin Gospel*, p. 140.

4 Alan Bennett, *Writing Home* ('Comfortable Words – An address to the Prayer Book Society on 12 May 1990') (London: Faber and Faber, 1994), p. 355.

Repentance

1 Florence Allshorn, *The Notebooks of Florence Allshorn* (London: SCM Press, 1957), pp. 20–1.

2 Maggie Ross, *The Fountain and the Furnace* (New York: Paulist Press, 1987), p. 121.

3 Marina Cantacuzino, *The Forgiveness Project* (London: Jessica Kingsley Publishers, 2016).

4 Richard Rohr, *Hope Against Darkness* (Cincinnati, OH: St Anthony Messenger Press, 2001), p. 73.

Choice

1 Richard Rohr, *The Naked Now* (New York: Crossroad, 2013), p. 86.

2 Rohr, *The Naked Now*, p. 88.

Week 5
Introduction

1 My own poem.

Lifestyle

1 Roland Walls, cited in *Celtic Daily Prayer* (London: Collins, 2015), p. 1411. Actual extract from Roland Walls, *Law and Gospel* (Oxford: SLG Press, 1980), used by permission.

Money

1 Justin Welby, *Dethroning Mammon* (London: Bloomsbury, 2016), p. 103.
2 Welby, *Dethroning Mammon*, p. 107.
3 Ghislaine Howard, 'Judas – The Departure', 8 April 2011, <http://ghislainehoward.com/judas-the-departure/>.

Pressure

1 Evelyn Underhill, *The Mount of Purification* (London: Longman, Green and Co., 1949), cited in *Celtic Daily Prayer Book 2* (London: Longman, Green & Co., 1949), p. 1576.
2 Claire Phipps and Sam Levin, '17 Confirmed Dead in "Horrific" Attack on Florida High School – As It Happened' *The Guardian*, 21 February 2018, <https://www.theguardian.com/us-news/live/2018/feb/14/florida-school-shooting-live-updates-latest-news-marjory-stoneman-douglas>.
3 Amanda Holpuch and Paul Owen, 'March for Our Lives: Hundreds of Thousands Demand End to Gun Violence – As It Happened', *The Guardian*, 24 March 2018, <https://www.theguardian.com/us-news/live/2018/mar/24/march-for-our-lives-protest-gun-violence-washington>.

Authenticity

1 Alan Bennett, *Writing Home* (London: Faber and Faber, 1994), p. 32.
2 Bennett, *Writing Home*, p. 42.

Trust

1 Robert Bridges, cited in Jennifer Wild and Hannah Ward (comp.), *The Lion Christian Quotation Collection* (Oxford: Lion, 1997), p. 204. Originally from *The Yattendon Hymnal*, first edition (1895), by permission of Oxford University Press.
2 Richard Rohr, *Falling Upward* (London: SPCK, 2012), p. xxvi.

Week 6

Introduction: pain

1 My own poem.
2 Samuel Wells, *Face to Face* (Norwich: Canterbury Press, 2019), p. 24.
3 Matthew Fox, *Original Blessing* (Rochester, VT: Bear and Co., 1983), pp. 141–3.
4 Walter Brueggemann, *The Prophetic Imagination*, heard in a lecture and paraphrased.

Weakness

1 Dag Hammarskjöld, cited in *The Lion Christian Quotation Collection* (Oxford: Lion, 1997), p. 263.
2 'Katharine Birbalsingh criticises failed education system', YouTube, 24 May 2011, <https://www.youtube.com/watch?v=XekkQ3HG2lg>.
3 *Why I Changed My Mind*, interview with Katharine Birbalsingh, BBC Radio 4, 25 October 2017.

Dislocation

1 William Shakespeare, *Hamlet*, Act 1, Scene 4.

Desolation

1 John of the Cross, cited in Jennifer Wild and Hannah Ward (comp.), *The Lion Christian Quotation Collection* (Oxford: Lion, 1997), p. 99.
2 Sheila Cassidy, *Light from the Dark Valley* (London: Darton, Longman and Todd, 1994), pp. 33–4.
3 Michael Hollings and Etta Gullick, *The One Who Listens* (Southend: Mayhew-McCrimmon, 1972), p. 144.
4 Eric Young, 'The Shack Defies Slump in Book Sales', *Christian Today*, 16 January 2009, <https://www.christiantoday.com/article/the.shack.defies.slump.in.book.sales/22323.htm>.

Prejudice

1 Maya Angelou, cited at <https://www.brainyquote.com/quotes/maya_angelou_148650>.
2 Peter B. Price, *The Things That Make for Peace* (London: Darton, Longman and Todd, 2018), p. 4; emphasis original.

Waiting

1 Jacques Ellul, *Hope in Time of Abandonment* (New York: Seabury Press, 1973), pp. 259, 396; emphasis original.

2 W. H. Vanstone, *The Stature of Waiting* (London: Darton, Longman and Todd, 1982), pp. 67–8.

After Easter
Miracle

1 Charles Harold Dodd, cited in Hannah Ward and Jennifer Wild (comp.), *The Lion Christian Quotation Collection* (Oxford: Lion, 1997), p. 251.

2 Jean Vanier, *The Gospel of John, The Gospel of Relationship* (London: Darton, Longman and Todd, 2016), p. 73.

Hope

1 Gerald Priestland, *Priestland's Progress* (London: BBC Books, 1983), p. 215.

2 *Believer*, BBC3, 7 October 2018.

3 *Church Times*, 12 October 2018.

4 Rubem A. Alves, *Tomorrow's Child* (London: SCM Press, 1972), pp. 194–6.

Joy

1 Teilhard de Chardin, cited at <https://www.goodreads.com/quotes/8986-joy-is-the-infallible-sign-of-the-presence-of-god>.

2 Friedrich von Hügel, *The Mystical Element of Religion* (London: J. M. Dent/James Clarke, 1908/1961), pp. 26–7.

Grace

1 Brennan Manning, cited at <https://www.goodreads.com/author/quotes/27405.Brennan_Manning?page=17>.

2 Ella Dove, 'From the Worst of Times . . . The Best of Us', *Good Housekeeping*, December 2017.

3 Gerard Manley Hopkins, cited in Hannah Ward and Jennifer Wild (comp.), *The Lion Christian Quotation Collection* (Oxford: Lion, 1997), p. 174.